Why Did You Do It?

Explanations for Offending by Young Offenders
in Their Own Words

Jackie Worrall

Why Did You Do It?
Explanations for Offending by Young Offenders in Their Own Words
Jackie Worrall

Published 2012 by
Waterside Press Ltd
Sherfield Gables
Sherfield on Loddon
Hook, Hampshire
United Kingdom RG27 0JG

Telephone +44(0)1256 882250
E-mail enquiries@watersidepress.co.uk
Online catalogue WatersidePress.co.uk

ISBN 978-1-904380-74-0 (Paperback)   **ISBN** 978-908162-08-3 (e-book)

Cataloguing-In-Publication Data A catalogue record for this book can be obtained on request from the British Library.

Cover design © 2012 Waterside Press. Design by www.gibgob.com

UK distributor Gardners Books, 1 Whittle Drive, Eastbourne, East Sussex, BN23 6QH. Tel: +44 (0)1323 521777; sales@gardners.com; www.gardners.com

North American distributor International Specialized Book Services (ISBS), 920 NE 58th Ave, Suite 300, Portland, Oregon, 97213, USA. Tel: 1 800 944 6190 Fax: 1 503 280 8832; orders@isbs.com; www.isbs.com

Printed by MPG-Biddles Ltd, Kings Lynn.

e-book *Why Did You Do It?* is available as an ebook and also to subscribers of Myilibrary and Dawsonera (for ISBN see above).

Why Did You Do It?

Explanations for Offending by Young Offenders
in Their Own Words

Jackie Worrall

Foreword Paul McDowell

CONTENTS

THE AUTHOR OF THE FOREWORD

Paul McDowell is Chief Executive of the crime reduction charity Nacro which he joined in 2009 following a career with HM Prison Service. During that time (and among other responsibilities over the years) he became Governor of Coldingley Prison in 2004 and of HM Prison Brixton in 2006. Earlier, in 2000, he was seconded from the Prison Service to the Home Office where he worked in the Prison Minister's Private Office.

FOREWORD

One thing we know for sure is that everyone has something to say about crime. Certainly there is no shortage of choice if you want to read about it. So what is the value of this particular contribution?

First of all it is worth considering the credentials of the author. In this case they are very impressive indeed. Having worked with offenders for four decades Jackie Worrall's knowledge and experience is unparalleled. Her experience as a criminal justice practitioner and as a respected commentator and policy thinker provide a compelling case to support the credentials of this book. On that basis alone there are few other books that can come close to being able to reflect the realities of the challenges we all face in criminal justice and particularly in relation to youth crime. It is also worth mentioning that few books on these issues come so close to young offenders themselves, offering a unique, first hand, insight into the thinking and motivations of young offenders.

This is an important book that is published at an important moment. It reflects the changing nature of the task of working with young offenders, and the challenge that is faced by criminal justice professionals in the public, voluntary and private sectors. And it reflects the nature of the new challenges set out by the Coalition government's 'rehabilitation revolution'. Certainly the insights outlined in the following pages about desistance from crime and barriers to that desistance have a clear resonance in relation to the 'rehabilitation revolution'.

But importantly in relation to solutions, the author makes it clear that it should not be about condoning or excusing crime. The issue is that the current punitive approach may not be the best way of dealing with it. Certainly the current drive to seek out alternative methodologies and financing arrangements, through the use of payment by results for instance, focuses on the responsibility of the individual offender, as well as shifting that for successfully reducing crime through working with individual offenders from the state to the provider.

Many of the solutions suggested in the book are rooted in practical intervention-focused ideas that are not new. And it will be fascinating to see if these common sense approaches can work if providers like Nacro are freed from historical constraints of having to bid for individual single issue contracts offered up by different government departments, in a singularly unplanned, unstructured and inconsistent way. For instance the book argues that we should do more to tackle the causes of crime and suggests family support and a welfare model so that we avoid having some young people who are seriously disadvantaged in comparison to others. The author makes the point that it is not inevitable that young men from poor backgrounds will offend, but at the same time we need to acknowledge that it is much easier to keep them out of trouble if you take a practical approach to solving common problems they face such as financial and emotional support from a family or from a mentor. Payment by results might provide the opportunity to take those practical solutions outlined in this very practical book and allow enlightened providers to join them up and deliver them to the right individual in the right place at the right time.

Dare we say it – joined up delivery of services might just be about to have its day. If that is to be the case then we should all pay attention to the messages provided by this book, and particularly by the young people quoted widely within it. There are valuable, reality based, practical lessons for all of us here. If we really do want to effectively reduce crime then we ignore those lessons at our peril.

Paul McDowell, Chief Executive, Nacro

THE AUTHOR

Dr Jackie Worrall was born in London and moved to the Midlands to read law at Warwick University. After graduating, she worked as a probation officer in Birmingham and in Warwickshire. In 1982 she joined Nacro, the crime reduction charity. Her first job there was as the manager of a youth training scheme and in a Nacro career of over 25 years she took on a variety of responsibilities, culminating in the role of Director of Policy and Public Affairs. She completed an MBA through the Open University and then an MA and PhD at Birmingham City University. She is married and lives in Leamington Spa.

ACKNOWLEDGEMENTS

This book would not have been written without the help of many people. I want to thank Waterside Press for accepting a proposal from a completely novice writer; Professor David Wilson for his encouragement and support; my husband for heroically reading the first drafts; and the staff at Nacro, some of whom helped with the interviews, for continuing to change lives and help young people despite cuts and crises.

Most importantly, my thanks go to the young men who have contributed to this book for so generously giving of their time and for sharing their thoughts and ideas.

The book was written to give them a voice. I hope it has done that and that the voice will be heard.

Jackie Worrall
January 2012

DEDICATION

For Brian, Richard, Phillip. Jules and Olivia with love.

INTRODUCTION

To help people be good rather than punish them for being bad.

Kate Atkinson, *Case Histories*, 2004.

Greg came very regularly to the training centre. He was learning painting and decorating and he had some aptitude for it. He was a likeable young man; tall and good looking he fitted the stereotype of the lovable rogue rather well. He had been a bit of a rogue. By the age of 17 he had racked up several convictions for theft. He was philosophical about the consequences and his, often repeated, advice to other trainees was *'If you can't do the time, don't do the crime'.*

We had been told that he lived with his father. His mother had died when Greg was a small child. He seemed to be making good progress and then one of the trainers noticed that he had a persistent and rather nasty cough. When she asked about it she found that he was worried because there was blood when he coughed. A doctor's appointment showed that our fears of serious illness were unfounded, he had strained a blood vessel in his throat. But we also learned that he was not living with his father; there had been an argument and he had left home. He was living by scavenging in dustbins in order to find food and was stealing from the local tip any items he could possibly sell on to get some money.

It is rarely right to take someone at face value and this is especially true of young offenders. All too often, behind the list of previous convictions, the exclusions from school, there has been neglect and abuse, poverty and disadvantage.

The young men in this book talk about home backgrounds in which violence and abuse were normal. They describe conflict with their parents and conflict in school. If we listen to what they are saying we will have to concede that they have had an unpromising start in life. We would have to accept that it has not been as easy for them to steer clear of crime as it is for young people who are fortunate enough to have adults who support, encourage and provide for them. We might agree that there should be some investment in help and support for children and families so that, one way or another, every child has a decent start in life. If we made that investment perhaps we would see fewer young people become involved in anti-social and criminal behaviour.

This book is not about making excuses for crime. It is about young men who have done both crime and time. It is less about where they have come from and more about where they are going, or at least where they are trying to go, because the remarkable fact is that most of these young men will stop committing crime. Most young offenders do grow up and grow out of it, despite the unpromising starts and despite their own mistakes.

The path to stopping is by no means a smooth one and, en route, the behaviour of young offenders may be far from attractive. Indeed many of the young men who speak here agree that their behaviour has been problematic, sometimes downright frightening. They accept that they have done wrong, they accept the fact of punishment. Now they are seeking a chance, at least, to be different.

These are not the gang leaders, the professional criminals, the predatory paedophiles; although some of these young men have been guilty of serious offences. These are boys who got into trouble and are now trying to find a way out of it. That is why most of them are taking part in prison education or participating in a training scheme or accepting the help of key workers and mentors. Many of the people who are working with them will know that, even when they are trying, progress can be slow, erratic and deeply frustrating. There seems to be an unwritten law that a crisis or another arrest comes just when everything seems to be going well. People who work with offenders also understand that it is not easy to change a way of life, to give up old mates and old habits, especially when, despite the best efforts to find somewhere decent to live or to get a job, there is rejection time after time after time. '*People judge you after prison*'.

Some 250 young offenders contributed to this book and, with only a tiny exception, they spoke of an intention to stop offending. They spoke about settling down, about getting qualifications, finding work, having a family. Some of them already know that these simple aspirations will be hard to achieve. Others will find out how hard it can be when they look for work and accommodation and find only discrimination and prejudice.

The names of these young men have been changed but the comments are their own. Their comments are sometimes crude, but they are sensitive, robust, practical and candid. The young men talk with openness and honesty about their lives and experiences and they are very clear about what contributed to their offending, what would help them to stop committing crime and what would make it much harder to leave crime behind. If we take the trouble to listen to what they say we might have a better understanding of why young men start to commit crime and what could be done to help them stop.

Instead of condemning out of hand we should be doing all we can to take down the barriers to desistance and to overcome the prejudice that so many young offenders face. We should stop punishing them for being bad and help them to be good.

Greg finished his basic painting and decorating training. He then went on a work placement with a local tradesman. After six months he was taken on as a full time employee. He has not been convicted of any other crimes.

CHAPTER ONE

SOME MORE EQUAL THAN OTHERS

The atrocious crime of being a young man ...

William Pitt, Earl of Chatham in a speech to the House of Commons, 1741.

He stood in the dock, unsmiling and insolent. He wore a grubby hoodie and torn jeans, which smelt of unwashed clothes and stale body odour. His hair was cropped very short so that the tattoo on his neck was visible. He was small for his age, which was 17. It was likely to be a prison sentence. The pre-sentence report was not encouraging and the solicitor had told him he was not likely to go home. It was street robbery this time: a serious offence.

His victim watched from the public seats. A smartly dressed woman in her mid-thirties, she looked at him through narrowed eyes and hoped he was going to pay for what he had done. It wasn't just that he had stolen her handbag. He had knocked her over, pushed her hard. She'd hurt her knee, ripped a hole in a nearly new pair of trousers. She'd cried. Her make up had run and she had felt embarrassed as well as shocked. She had been listening to her iPod and had noticed nothing until she felt the shove. The policeman made her feel stupid for not paying more attention and for trying to hang on to her bag. She'd had to take time off work to come to court and give evidence. Now she could be sitting next to all his friends and family for all she knew; all turned up to cheer him on!

That at least was not a problem. He had no family who would come to court to offer any kind of support.

He was one of five children living in a terraced house quite close to the city centre. The house was small and a bit damp. Not enough room for everyone, especially since his sister got pregnant and there was a baby in the place. His older brothers weren't always there, usually because they were doing time themselves. No one in the house had any work and when he started school he soon found he was getting himself up and out the door. He hated school. The teachers talked down to him and they wrote stuff on

17

the blackboard that he couldn't see properly. By the time he'd worked out what it said it had been rubbed off. He got into trouble for cheeking the teacher and then for fighting. His mum and step-dad went up to the school and that made it worse because his step-dad threw a wobbly and the school said they would get the police if he didn't calm down. Of course he got a beating at home for being trouble at school. In the end he walked out of home. *'Just one too many beatings'.*

He had no money and nowhere to go, so he was sofa surfing with some mates and sleeping rough when he couldn't find anything else. There was no hope of getting a job or even getting any sort of benefit without an address. He saw this woman with her bag on her arm and she wasn't paying any attention so he thought it would be dead easy to grab it. How was he to know she would try to hang on to the bag. He'd done plenty of stuff before but never hurt anyone like that. This time it would be custody. He'd heard stories about that from his brothers and some of his mates. He was scared, but not going to show that to anyone. *'Let them think I'm hard'.*

This book is about the young men who find themselves in the dock, sometimes for serious offences. It uses their words and ideas to try to explain why some young people get into trouble with the police and how circumstances often conspire to make the consequences of early mistakes disproportionate for some of them. It aims to show why some young people offend and why they stop offending. It is not seeking absolution for them nor is it denying that criminal behaviour is unattractive and unacceptable. The costs to victims may also be disproportionate.

What the book does seek to do is to encourage a response to youth crime that is not based on emotional responses, tabloid headlines and misperceptions about the behaviour of young people. Because, only when we properly understand and accept some of the reasons that young people commit crimes are we likely to be able to tackle the problem of youth offending and manage it effectively. Much of the research literature quoted is not new and many of the comments from the young offenders themselves echo what will be familiar messages for people who work with offenders. It is all the more poignant that the messages, clear and consistent though they remain, still go largely unheard. The voices of these young offenders should add weight to such messages and strengthen the case for a radical rethink of youth crime and youth justice in the United Kingdom.

To be the victim of crime is to be on the receiving end of a very unpleasant experience. No one wants to be such a victim, even a relatively minor one. So it is hardly surprising that there is considerable fear of crime. But while we fear crime we are also strangely fascinated by it. Every bookshop has shelves full of true crime stories as well as masses of crime fiction. We lap up stories about criminals, policemen, detectives and lawyers, from Hercule Poirot to Inspector Morse from Cracker to Midsomer Murders. We even get to like some of the crooks and criminals if they are suitably colourful, like Captain Jack Sparrow. While we read with enjoyment the exploits of the fictional rogues and their fictional pursuers we read about crime in our newspapers and magazines and are outraged by stories of senseless killing and traumatised victims.

We are ambivalent about crime. Jack Sparrow is one of many 'lovable rogues' who turn up in history and in fiction. We enjoy the exploits of Dick Turpin. Who is going to dislike Butch Cassidy and the Sundance Kid after they have seen Paul Newman and Robert Redford bring them to a cinema near you? Nor can we assume that the average citizen is entirely law abiding, though most will never be convicted of a crime. What about the person who brings home the stationery from the office or those who inflate the insurance claim? Outside of the criminal law there can be few drivers who have never broken the law; parking on a double yellow line may not be a heinous crime but we are at greater risk of being killed by a careless, speeding driver than by a serial killer.

In 2010, James McGuire pointed out that people's fear of crime is likely to be out of proportion to the 'objective' risk of becoming a victim of it. He suggested that this may be partly because of media attention and sensationalism. One Home Office study, completed by Lovbakke in 2007, found that readers of national tabloid newspapers are twice as likely as those who read national broadsheets to think that crime has significantly increased in recent years both locally and nationally. A report published by the Institute for Public Policy Research (IPPR) in 2008 includes some analysis of the *British Crime Survey* which reveals that in 2004-2005 more than 1.5 million people in Britain had thought about leaving their local area because of young people hanging around and 1.7 million said that they avoided going out after dark as a direct result.

This fear, this fascination, this ambivalence is all understandable but there is danger in it. There is a risk that we conflate all sorts of crime, mixing up the petty offending of a vulnerable teenager with the serious or violent crime committed by a professional criminal. The IPPR report comments on the concerns about young people being present in public spaces, apparently seeing persistent graffiti or young people hanging around as more of a threat to local safety than burglary. Crime statistics do not always reveal the discrepancy between crimes that may carry the same name, so a street robbery might be the violent mugging of an elderly woman or two teenagers fighting over a mobile phone or a coat. We read about serious crime in the newspaper and it is easy to forget that these serious, often tragic, crimes are mercifully rare. The crimes that we are more likely to see and, perhaps, to experience are more likely to be petty and mundane. They may still be a profound nuisance but they are neither life threatening nor newsworthy.

The result of this conflation is that when someone is labelled as an 'offender', a 'criminal' there is no immediate distinction between a determined, possibly professional, adult offender and a child or young person who has been reckless and made some mistakes and so the way that we, as a society, expect this offender to be dealt with is based on very little understanding, knowledge or experience.

There is no question that a lot of crime is committed by young people, mostly by young men. Crime may be said to be a young man's game. However, this should not be a reason to demonise young people and to assume that all of them are threat to society as a whole and to us as individuals. Most young people are not young offenders. Most young people are law abiding, likely to be more concerned with passing their exams and getting on with their lives than with committing crime. Yet many of them speak of the hostility they encounter from adults, the poor service they get from shop assistants, the way in which they are told, often quite rudely, to get out of the way or to turn their music down. Sixteen year old Dan commented

> I went into this shop to get a present for my mum. It was her birthday. They just
> didn't serve me. There were two women there talking and they took no notice of

me at all. I could have done with a bit of help deciding what mum might like but they certainly weren't going to give me any.

Police officers and local councils routinely deal with complaints about young people 'hanging around on the streets'. These are usually not young people who are doing anything wrong but who are simply socialising. It may be loud and boisterous and they may be in the way so it might be something of a nuisance, but to see young people enjoying themselves as a threat provides a disturbing perspective on adult attitudes.

Writing in 1999 John Muncie commented on the hostility towards and fear of youth and noted,

> Youth and adolescents usually conjure up a number of emotive and troubling images. These range from notions of uncontrolled freedom, irresponsibility, vulgarity, rebellion and dangerousness to those of deficiency, vulnerability, deprivation or immaturity.

One young man commented

> We were always getting into trouble. Not doing anything like but just hanging around by the bus shelter having a bit of a laugh. Where else can you go? There's nowhere round our way but as soon as you stand there with a crowd of mates there they are. 'Move along please'.

Another was critical of the attitude of security staff in the shopping mall

> We hang around there sometimes because it's a place to go. It's warm. Out of the weather. But you just stand there and they come along and tell you to get out. As if you're going to rob all the shops.

There is nothing new about the tendency to treat young people with dislike and distrust. The term 'hooligan' became part of the English language in the late 1800s and Muncie comments on a report compiled by the Howard Association on Juvenile Offenders in 1898 which gave the general impression that young people were 'becoming increasingly unruly, more vulgar and undisciplined'. One hundred years later the *Daily Express*, leader column quoted by Vivien Stern in 1998 read 'At one time our image of youthful callousness and cruelty was of children amusing themselves by pulling the wings off flies. Not any more. Who are they, these monsters who now prowl our streets? Simple. They are our children'.

It is understandable on some levels that adults fear crime and so young people as potential perpetrators, though the perception of 'monsters prowling the streets' seems rather excessive. David Cameron tells us that we have a 'broken Britain'. Tony Blair describing his 'journey' remarks that he had held the view that crime was widespread and often organized. It was late in his tenure as Prime Minister that he appears to have realised that this is not the case. Most people he found were not criminal, in the sense that we usually use the term. He became aware that most young people are law abiding and it is only a minority who give rise to concern. If our leading politicians are unaware of the true levels of crime among young people it is hardly surprising that those of us with less access to the facts and statistics should have a range of misperceptions about the whole issue.

It should be a priority to overcome these misperceptions. Only when we accept a rational view of youth crime can we find ways to prevent involvement in crime wherever possible and, when that is not possible, find ways to discourage re-offending. An effective solution makes good sense economically. Preventing crime has some resource implications for sure but there is nothing that costs as much as picking up the pieces through a criminal justice model where the ultimate penalty, a prison sentence, costs an average of £45,000 per year per place.

There are many theories about why young people commit crime. There are also many theories about why they stop. All of these suggest that there are many different reasons why a young person may get into trouble with the law. There is, however, a strong consensus about the factors that make it more likely that a young person is at risk of offending. There are also factors which influence the likelihood of arrest and conviction and theories that suggest why some young people are more vulnerable to earning the 'young offender' label. That there is a strong consensus, views consistent over many years, should surely suggest that we do have ideas about what would work in preventing youth crime. If we know that there are factors that increase the risk should we not address those and, as a consequence, divert young people from crime. Much of the consensus focuses on factors outside of the criminal justice system and a punishment approach and yet we continue to rely on the punishment model. To quote one Prime Minister, if we are going to be 'tough on crime, tough on the causes of crime' we need, to paraphrase another one 'to understand a little more and condemn a little less'. Indeed it seems entirely reprehensible that a Prime Minister could suggest that a response to crime should be based on anything other than a full understanding of the problem, although that is what John Major's original statement implied.

These days market research is regularly used to determine what services are wanted or needed. If we are trying to develop a new car design, build a new office block or open a new shop we might conduct a survey to make sure that the product is right for the potential market. It would be important to find out if the idea is financially viable, if it will be used, if there is already serious competition in the area. We would ask potential customers. We do not generally ask young people who have committed offences why they did it, why they stopped, what would help them stop and what gets in the way of desisting from offending. When we do ask the questions we seem all too rarely to listen to the answers.

This is understandable too. Anyone living with a teenage boy will appreciate the tendency to communicate, using the term loosely, in occasional nods and grunts. There is a substantial amount of literature to support the view that young men will not willingly share their worries or show their emotions. Askew and Ross, for example, in their study 'Boys Don't Cry; Boys and Sexism in Education' published in 1988 quoted Sean who said,

> You have to be careful about what you let out about yourself. You get picked on for anything around here. You've got to be careful not to let the other kids think you're soft.

The 'stiff upper lip' remains with us in the need to be seen as hard and strong. More than this it is likely that the young men who do become offenders will be among the least articulate, the least able to express worries and fears and the least able to engage in any sort of constructive dialogue with authority figures.

In 2001, Stephen Shaw, the then Prisons and Probation Ombudsman, commented on the dearth of complaints he had received from young men in young offender institutions. While he stated that he had no wish to encourage a complaints culture he was concerned that those with genuine complaints might simply lack the skills to express them.

So, while there are, inevitably, exceptions to the rule, young offenders tend not to say much about their reasons for offending and are not likely to be eloquent on the subject of the causes of crime. When they do comment, however, the comments are likely to be revealing.

One young man who contributed to a report produced by Nacro in 1999 said:

> All it boils down to a reason why people get bad and that is through their parents and it is partly down to them as well but the environment they're brought up in … you see kids, like posh kids and that, you don't see them going out and doing crime and that. They live in a posh area, they don't know people from where I live, they live in a posh area they don't know no criminals, none at all. It's all to do with that, and you know parents, how you get brought up and by what standards.

Another commented:

> I had people say to me, yeah, it's your fault you're in jail but it isn't my fault. I'm the one that was slung out of my home eleven years of age, no mum to love me, no dad to love me, no brothers nothing. I had to go out in the big wide world to fight for myself, to find clothes for myself and all this … You get Social Services, yeah, but they don't give you nothing, nothing at all. What do they give you? Nothing. It's the mothers and fathers fault that's all. It's the love your family has to give you that can stop (offending) nothing else, nothing else. If your mum and dad shows you neglect at all I guarantee you're going into crime.

This book gives young offenders the chance to say, in their own words, what leads to involvement in crime and why, for most of them, that involvement comes to an end. Not all of them are able to be eloquent but they do have ideas and theories of their own about the reasons why young men get into trouble. They also talk about the problems that young offenders are faced with when they do try to change their lifestyle, even when they are genuinely trying to leave crime behind. Many of them accept that, ultimately, the decision to desist from crime is a personal decision and many accept responsibility for their mistakes and for their situation. None the less they describe circumstances which make it very hard indeed to lead a different sort of life.

The book is based on interviews with young offenders, some of whom are in custody. Some of those taking part in the interviews had committed serious offences though the majority of the comments come from young men whose criminal activity is relatively minor.

There is extensive literature that explores the nature of the young offender and the concept of youth crime. A substantial amount of the evidence has come from the Cambridge study, a longitudinal study of young men conducted by David Farrington and Donald West but the study is far from being the only source of information about youth crime and young offenders. Rutter, Giller and Hagel (1998), Smith (1995) and Muncie (1999) are among the many writers and researchers who comment on the phenomenon and suggest theoretical perspectives and explanations. There is no single theory that explains fully why some young men commit crime. How could there be when there are numerous explanations that might account for the development of anti-social and criminal behaviour?

Explanations range from a series of environmental and situational factors to the proposition that there is a recognisable criminal type. There is also some debate about what constitutes a 'young offender'. Is it simply someone who has been caught and convicted? John Muncie points out that self reported crime studies conclude that offending is more common among young men than many people believe. Very few young people say that they have never done anything wrong. Andrew Rutherford (1995) has similarly suggested that some level of criminal behaviour is relatively normal among adolescent young men but also argues that the responses to that behaviour from parents, school and police can make the difference between just growing out of it and becoming more deeply involved in crime; becoming labelled as an offender.

Rutherford also suggests that there is a spectrum of offending behaviour among young men. At one end of the spectrum are those young men who may be guilty of some anti-social behaviour, usually committing only petty crime from which they desist as they reach maturity. At the other end of that spectrum are those young men whose anti-social behaviour has been marked from a very early age and it is these who may be more at risk of offending into adulthood. At this end of the spectrum Farrington (1996), Rutherford (1995) and Rutter, Giller and Hagel (1998), among others, suggest that there are likely to be characteristics and extremes of behaviour that are beyond the bounds of adolescent normality. Those concerned are more likely to have displayed unruly behaviour from an early age and to have had difficulty in developing relationships not only with adults but also with other children. While there is little to distinguish the identified petty offender from the apparent non-offender this group will display characteristics that are different from both petty offenders and non-offenders.

The majority of young offenders will start their offending as they reach their teens. Why? First there is the impact of adolescence, a time of some turbulence for many young people. It is a time of change. Emler and Reicher (1995) pointed out that at the start of adolescence school is central to a young person's life and by the end they may be looking to the job market and the trappings of adulthood. For most young people there will be enormous changes in their expectations, interests and ideas. There will be changes in themselves too as they grow and mature, some more rapidly than others. Many theorists, including Justice (1996) and Keating (1990) agree that there is a change in thinking processes during adolescence, part of which involves the development of a sense of consequence. It is still unformed during adolescence and so there is a greater likelihood of reckless behaviour. This is likely to be more the case for those young people who are slow to mature.

The psychoanalytical school has contributed significantly to the literature concerning adolescence. Anna Freud (1952) ascribed the turmoil of adolescence to a need to deal with the guilt that arises from awakening sexuality. This guilt, she argued, leads to a need to be rebellious and to challenge parental rules and expectations. Eriksen (1968) saw an association between this rebellion and non-conforming behaviour and the developing identity. He suggested that it is the fragility of the young man's identity as it develops that leads to a need to challenge and test it by rebellious behaviour. He argued that the development of identity during adolescence, the achievement of psychosocial well-being and a sense of knowing where one is going is crucial. He further argued that a supportive and communicative family life is likely to create an environment in which the adolescent can resolve identity crisis. Conversely, poor communication and poor bonding with parents is likely to result in feelings of insecurity and inadequate identity formation. Adolescence is the time when a young person starts to seek independence from their family and wants to develop an identity of their own. This can involve some rebellion and some trauma. It is certainly likely to contribute to conflict with parents. This may be challenging but manageable in a household where parents are confident about their own identity and values but can lead to conflict which rapidly gets out of hand in an environment where communication is generally poor and the fundamental bond between parent and child is weak. Where parents are not able to provide support the young person is more exposed to the influence of others and where those others are themselves anti-social there is a vulnerability to an anti-social identity. Marcia (1966) and Walsh (1982) both argued that the child who lacks stability and adult role models has less opportunity to develop the values and ethics that guide and restrain behaviour. Where, after all, do any of us learn right from wrong if it is not from responsible adults in our lives?

In 1990 Coleman and Hendry suggested that role conflict and identity crisis is inevitable as the adolescent struggles to meet the various expectations of parents, teachers, peers and girlfriends. Nor are the changes all in the mind. Rutherford (1995) suggested that there was a link with the growth spurts, common in teenage boys, and that it is likely that the dramatic physical changes experienced by the adolescent boy would be mirrored by emotional and psychological change. The concept of the stormy adolescence is not without its challengers, not every young person becomes anti-social at the age of 13. None the less it is a time of great change and it may be that the young offender is disproportionately affected by the changes because of a lack of parental understanding and because they are often without the support of a school environment and more positive peer relationships. Rutter et al (1979) comment that social circumstances affect intellectual development. For most young people any delinquency is a passing phase but when it is associated with other factors it may become more prolonged so the rebellion and conflict often associated with adolescence, exacerbated by poor parenting and a destabilised home life, may become extended and more serious.

Nor is it just adolescence which gives rise to potential behavioural problems. There may also be a connection with just being male. There is a significant body of research that suggests that traditional male values and attitudes may be highly relevant. Adolescent girls do commit crimes and do behave in anti-social ways but it is boys who dominate the criminal justice system and the prison population. So what is it about boys?

Many writers have suggested that the traditional view of masculinity involves dominance, control and independence, making it less likely that boys will be willing to conform to rules set by others in authority and so less compliant in school and in relationships with authority figures. There has certainly been concern that boys under perform in school because it is important, socially, not to be seen to be working hard and to be taking school work seriously, not to be seen as 'the swot' or 'the boffin'. Askew and Ross (1988) have also commented on the unwillingness of boys to be open about their emotions or to listen sympathetically to the comments of others.

John Head, writing in 1999 commented on the behaviour of boys in groups; suggesting that they constantly bicker, interrupting and challenging each other. Head also comments that they act out mock fights and talk in a competitive way with each speaker more interested in asserting his own views than in listening to anyone else. For many young men their masculinity is associated with toughness, and demonstrations of toughness can easily escalate into physical demonstration of being tough and being hard. Young offenders themselves have commented that one reason for getting into trouble is that there is a need to look hard in front of their mates. The same need to be tough makes it harder to be the one who says 'no' when there is a suggestion of reckless behaviour. Few boys will take the risk of being seen as the wimp by avoiding a situation that may even be potentially dangerous. It takes a great deal of self-confidence to be the only member of a group that does not take part in a shared activity. Few adolescents have that degree of confidence. In 1964 Matza suggested that young men seek to exhibit their manhood through misbehaviour and this was endorsed in 1977 by Willis who described the notion of masculinity displayed by his 'lads'; based on crime and toughness; while they were scathing about the hardworking 'earoles'.

For the unemployed young man, living in a deprived city area, the excitement of crime offers an emotional charge and reflects identification with a tough masculinity. In this context joy-riding and ram-raiding can be seen as manifestations of aggressive masculinity. In 1998 Collier suggested that persistent offending among some young men may relate to the continuing need to present as tough and strong. Those who do not walk the thin line between danger and conformity are subject to criticism within the traditional male culture.

Young men are expected to get up to mischief. Jefferson (1982) suggested that the 'boy who never walked on the wild side is suspect'. Certainly there is some ambiguity in our expectations of boys. 'Boys will be boys' after all. Indeed it might be argued that the reason that young women who offend are treated with some abhorrence is because crime is seen as something quintessentially male. Sandra Walklate (1995) suggested that boys learn to be offenders and to adopt a conventional masculinity. Less controlled by social convention than adolescent girls they learn from each other to be tough, active and risk taking. They are more often out on the streets where the potential to become involved in crime, as well as to become a victim of it, is great. In Canaan's (1996) study the sample group was unemployed, low skilled and pessimistic about their futures. Apparently without the opportunity to prove themselves as men by finding stable employment they resorted to drinking and fighting as a means to assert their masculinity.

So it may be that among adolescent boys there is some predisposition towards mischief at the very least. The consequences for some boys may, however, be very different. Following the publication of the Barrow Cadbury Commission report 'Lost in Transition', Barrow Cadbury led an initiative 'Transition to Adulthood' which drew attention to the fact that for young people with functional middle class families there is support in place for the young person right through childhood and adolescence and into adulthood. The child who stays on at school and then goes on to higher education will have support, sometimes a considerable amount of it, until they are at least 21-years-old. The young person who does not have parental support, who has been excluded from school, may be living alone and independently while still little more than a child. Rutherford (1995) stressed the importance of 'holding on' to young people until they 'grow out of crime'. This may not be an easy task. Parents who have experienced the trials and tribulations of the teenage boy will acknowledge that the period is littered with conflict and argument but the difference between the family who try to manage the, sometimes, difficult behaviour and the parent who gives up on their child is significant. One young offender remarked *I've been on the streets since I was 14. My mum chucked me out*.

In the 1970s, Chambliss made a comparison between two groups of young men who he called the Saints and the Roughnecks. The Saints got up to their fair share of mischief. They drank to excess, they committed crimes. The Saints were of a middle class background and they could do much of their drinking or drug-taking in the privacy of parental homes. They had cars and so they could travel to different places where they would not be known or recognized. In the event that they did get caught for any misbehaviour they had the social skills to be suitably sheepish and apologetic. As a consequence they were not often caught misbehaving and, when they were, they were able to disarm authority sufficiently to ensure that they were not excluded from school, charged with offences or thrown out of home. As they became adult they stopped the reckless behaviour, the excesses and the crime and became responsible adults.

In contrast the Roughnecks had neither parental support nor parental money behind them. They were more likely to congregate on the street so that they, and their misdemeanours, were more visible. They did not have transport so they tended to hang around in the same places where they were recognised and often picked up by the police. If they were challenged about their behaviour they were more likely to become aggressive and confrontational sparking off more hostile responses from the authority figures in their lives. They were more likely, therefore, to be excluded from school, to be arrested and charged and to end up with a criminal record. Predictably the majority of the group went on to commit further criminal offences and to serve prison sentences.

This suggests that family background may be of extreme importance not just in preventing young people from getting involved in crime at all but also in preventing the consequences of wild behaviour and adolescent mistakes from becoming consequences that will impact on them for the rest of their lives.

It can be argued that this is hardly surprising. The family is the starting point for most of us. It is the place where, when all is well, children are loved, corrected if they do wrong, given a sense of values and provided with the emotional and practical help that we all need in childhood. What happens when the family cannot or will not provide that?

In 1996, David Farrington produced a report for the Joseph Rowntree Foundation in which he identified a number of risk factors, which may predict offending, related to the family. Harsh, lax or erratic parenting, family dysfunction, criminal members of the family, interference from other family members in the child's upbringing. The Institute for Public Policy Research (IPPR) report 'Make Me A Criminal' (2008) similarly identified 'Having a parent who is an offender, poor relations with parents and not spending much time with parents' as one of the risk factors for offending.

Parents and family provide the first steps in becoming socialised for most children. It is in the family that the child learns how to deal with other people, learns what behaviour is rewarded and what incurs some sort of penalty. It is in the family that children are prepared in every way for going to school for the first time. They learn in advance how to relate to teachers and to peers. In a family where, for whatever reason, their questions go unanswered, naughtiness is unchallenged and good behaviour goes unrewarded how can they learn the behaviour that will be accepted in school? Unprepared for school they misbehave, they are challenged by teachers, they do not cope well with the challenge so that teachers see them as rude or aggressive and a spiral of hostility develops, often leading to ultimate exclusion from school. Tragically, for many young offenders this is not simply a matter of a family in which there is a limited amount of care, often there is abuse, physical, emotional or sexual. One young man spoke of sleeping with a knife under his pillow because he was so terrified of his stepfather.

On this basis it is all too easy to lapse into blaming parents. Sometimes that may be justified. Who could possibly excuse a parent or step parent for so terrifying a child that they felt they needed protection? On the other hand there will be families who do try to do what they can for their children but are just not able to cope. Poverty, mental health issues, bereavement or other trauma might all make a difference to whether parents are able to care for the children as they should and they themselves might wish. In some

31

families the difficulties may be temporary, caused by an unexpected event such as redundancy or post-natal depression. For some parents there will never have been a role model to show them what 'good parenting' means. The importance of this has been increasingly recognised over the years and there are parenting courses available. Sadly they are not always easy to access for those parents who might need the help most.

Attendance and progress in school is also likely to be relevant to potential offending. Many writers have made links between school failure and offending. It is less clear whether this is because of low intelligence and a lack of ability to think in abstract terms or because of school failure itself, but it is not unreasonable to assume that if school is an unpleasant experience for a boy he will not succeed readily. Farrington (1996) identified low intelligence as a key factor. He cites Statten and Klinkeberg-Larsen's (1990) study of 120 young men from Stockholm in which low intelligence measured at age three significantly predicted officially recorded offending up to the age of 30. Farrington and West's own study in 1973 also showed that twice as many boys scoring 90 or less in a non-verbal intelligence test at the age of eight were convicted as juveniles than those scoring higher. Farrington (1973) also considers whether it is the inability to manipulate abstract concepts and the limited ability to foresee consequences which are the true correlates of crime or whether it is school failure. Maughn et al (1996) found evidence that the correlate was school failure. Hirshci (1969) had also suggested a direct relationship between school failure and lack of attachment to school and delinquency. He argued that it would be surprising if there were not a relationship between academic competence and a tendency to drop out of the institution in which that competence was of supreme importance. It may also be that the experience is so negative that it creates barriers to learning even for the more able child. A large group of young offenders spoke of the very poor relationships they had had with their teachers and commented that they received little support or encouragement. For the child who starts out by inviting the hostility of teachers and who may be hyperactive and impulsive, the traditional concepts of teaching in large groups and in an environment that requires a level of compliance and concentration may be rather doomed to failure. The consequences of school failure set off another spiral. Exclusion from school is a missed opportunity to be involved in the socialising aspect of the institution. It also means few, if any, qualifications, which make it harder to find work. Failure to find work makes it less easy to afford somewhere decent to live. All of these factors have a cumulative effect, building disadvantage on disadvantage and making the child more vulnerable to involvement in crime.

Despite all this, most of those who become involved in crime will stop when they become adults. In many cases there will have been some form of intervention. Involvement in the criminal justice system may have brought with it some help in finding a job, developing skills, finding somewhere to live. Some young offenders will have completed courses that will help in managing anger, dealing with addiction or improving reasoning and thinking skills. Some will have learned to read for the first time because of education in prison and some will have had time to reflect. All of this may be part of a rehabilitation programme and young offenders will often acknowledge that this will have helped them and given them the chance to make a change in their lifestyle.

Some young people will have unacknowledged help through their family or their friends. Some will have a specific reason to change: a new relationship, becoming a parent, moving to a new area, getting the job or flat and having something worth keeping. The uncertainty is whether it is the rehabilitation that makes the difference or whether there is a point, or a series of points, in the lives of young men when they begin to desist from crime. Many young offenders would say that this is the critical element. The individual has to want to stop and to be prepared to make the effort to stop. No amount of help can prevent a person from committing offences if that is what they still want to do.

This is not an argument for doing nothing. Youth offending causes distress and damage. It has to be dealt with. Young offenders themselves acknowledge that if someone does go wrong then there is a need to punish them for it. However, it does need to be a fair punishment and one which takes fully into account the factors that may have led to an involvement in crime and the commission of any particular crime. It is not about being soft on crime or those that commit it but rather about managing crime and its consequences in a rational and effective way.

Charles Dickens understood. When Rose Maylie sees Oliver Twist for the first time and is told he is responsible for the attempted burglary of her home she says,

> But even if he has been wicked think how young he is; think he may never have known a mother's love, or the comfort of a home, that ill usage and blows, or the want of bread, may have driven him to herd with men who have forced him to guilt. Aunt, dear aunt, for mercy's sake, think of this, before you let them drag this sick child to prison, which in any case must be the grave of all his chances of amendment. Oh! As you love me and know that I have never felt the want of parents in your goodness and affection, but that I might have done so, and might have been equally helpless and unprotected with this poor child, have pity on him before it is too late.

The theories and the evidence about the causes of crime and desistance from it are far from new. The comments made here by young people are also taken from a period of over ten years. Their concerns and the possible solutions they suggest are, significantly, the same. Most of these young offenders acknowledge that they have done wrong, some have committed serious crimes and have caused serious hurt to others. They accept that there must be some consequence, some punishment for that. Many of these young men have also been the victim of circumstances, they have not been well looked after by their parents, they have not had support form their school or from any other institution. Some of them have made mistakes, not always very serious mistakes, which have had disproportionate consequences affecting their whole lives.

The great majority of the young men involved in this book want to stop offending for one reason or another. Many of them, though, will find that this is very much easier said than done. They will find that the fact of a criminal record closes doors which have to be open if they are to have any chance at all of leading a law abiding life.

It has been well known for many years that the use of custody is an expensive, and often ineffective, way of dealing with crime. The cuts of October 2010 reducing both Home Office and Ministry of Justice budgets by 23% gave further reason to think seriously and radically about the ways in which crime can be prevented and re-offending managed. There are cheaper and possibly more effective solutions for the politicians brave enough to defy the tabloid press and take a rational approach to the management of crime.

This book will offer no magic bullets. It is not going to suggest a single way to eradicate crime. What it will suggest is that young offenders themselves can often recognise that their behaviour has been problematic and that they have done wrong; they can also see what would help them to behave differently and they know what barriers there are that will make it very hard for them to behave any differently. It is high time that we gave proper attention to what they have to say.

CHAPTER TWO

BRAVADO, BULLYING AND BOREDOM

The man who makes no mistakes does not usually make anything.

Edward John Phelps, Speech at Mansion House, 24 January 1899.

There is voluminous research literature about the causes of youth crime. This consistently points to the relevance of physical attributes such as hyperactivity, impulsiveness (often called impulsivity) and limited ability to understand the consequences of actions and their impact on other people. There is similar consistency about the external factors that increase the risks of involvement in crime including inappropriate parenting, school failure and a disadvantaged urban background.

Also consistent with the theoretical perspectives are the comments and insights of young offenders themselves. In December 2010 the *Guardian* (8 December 2010) reported on an event organized through User Voice. This event gave young offenders the opportunity to give their views on cutting crime. Policy makers and politicians involved in the event described themselves as shocked by the insight and sensitivity shown by the young people involved and by the fact that they were solution-focused and not just there to complain about their lot. All the more of a concern then that there has been little evidence of listening to their comments or to those of the academics whose findings support those views.

There was a remarkable consistency between the comments made by that group of offenders to those of other young offenders made over the last few years. In a series of interviews and discussions some 250 young offenders have added their comments to the long-running debate about the causes of crime and the reasons for desistance.

Boredom was seen by many of them as a significant factor; young people with nothing to do and nowhere to go using the excitement of crime as an antidote to boredom and frustrations. One group of young men were very much in agreement about the lack of opportunity for legitimate fun and excitement.

Linden's comment highlights the problem of being out on the streets:

> There is nothing to do. Everyone is in the same boat. You meet up outside the shops. You are just there when things happen. You can stand on the corner and see all sorts of things.

Brady simply stated,

> Kids get bored, they do it for fun.

His friend, Steven, agreed, saying,

> It's the youngsters, there's nothing to do.

Both Mark and Lee commented on the excitement of being chased and of the thrill of doing something that you should not be doing.

> Adrenalin. Committing crime, getting chased, there's an adrenalin rush that feels good'

> It's good to get a chase and there's a buzz about doing stuff that's bad.

Thomas's comment demonstrates that it is sometimes more than just boredom. It is also about being part of the group and either being pushed into doing something wrong but exciting or getting involved because you don't want to be the one who is left out.

> Boys get into trouble because there is nothing to do; just hanging around. It's who you hang around with. People follow a leader and get bullied into doing things. If you haven't got many friends it's hard to say no.

A significant number of young offenders suggested that offending was about 'fun', counteracting boredom and the problem of hanging around on the streets. Boredom also led to substance use in order to get a high.

'Boredom. Nothing to do but drink and take drugs.'

Drink was seen to be a major factor; David said that for him it was partly boredom but also not really thinking straight.

Being bored. Nothing to do. Being stupid. Taking stupid decisions when pissed.'

Simmy used drugs and alcohol as well as crime for his excitement.

There's nothing to do except drugs, alcohol and shoplifting.

Lack of local facilities for young people was also seen as the reason for boredom and for problems.

There's no facilities, only a baby park. There is a youth club now but it's only for under twelves'

The kids have nothing to do. You sit in a flat all day and watch TV.

Having nothing to do and nowhere to go also leads to increased visibility and becoming recognised by the police. Some young offenders thought that police responses created further problems. In some cases it was quite simply, 'Don't like the police' but others spoke of the 'police antagonising areas and groups'.

One young man commented on the problem of being noticed.

Hanging around in large groups of youths and attracting attention from the police.

Some groups also attracted more attention than others. Darren was still angry about his experiences.

39

> They used to take liberties. They were horrible. Pick us up, throw us in the van. 'Don't move you black bastard'. It just made us so angry. It enforced my hatred, at the time, of white people.

There is evidence that the reason that young black men are so much over-represented in the prison system is not because they are more likely to offend. It is rather because they are more likely to be stopped and searched, arrested, charged, convicted and remanded in custody and to receive a custodial sentence than their white counterparts (Nacro 1986, 1989; Hood 1992).

Although it was suggested 'the police have too much power' there were relatively few who actively blamed the police. There was a general awareness that hanging around on the street leaves you vulnerable to accusations of doing something worse. While there is a real issue about where young people can go to meet, when they are too old, and probably too cynical for the youth clubs and too young for the pubs there was recognition that the choice of people to hang around with is highly relevant. Peer pressures were very important. It was important not to be the one who walked away when trouble started and some commented on the fact of showing off and posturing to maintain credibility in a group or gang. Grant and Steven both commented on the need to show off.

> They want attention. Peer pressures. Problems they have.

> They think it's fun to break the law, then show off to their mates.

Not just to their mates either, according to Arif.

> There was a little gang of us. We were all the same. Showing off in front of the girls.

Pete wasn't sure why some of his friends had got into trouble but he too thought that showing off was part of the problem:

> They want to make themselves look big. I've got lots of mates in trouble. Don't even know why.

Just happens through socialising with the wrong peer group.

The last comment above was David's. This was endorsed by Mustafa, who was sure that the reasons for his getting into trouble were 'the environment I was in and the crowd I went with'. Ian said,

I know it sounds as though I am looking for someone to blame but it was the kids who I went round with who got me into crime.

Paul commented,

Hanging with the wrong people. Getting dragged in to doing missions, like doing houses over.

'Getting into groups, peer pressure, getting new friends and stupidity' were the reasons that Grant gave for getting into trouble and many of the comments confirmed that the need to go along with the crowd was of major importance for many young men as all of the following comments suggest.

People that you hang around with can get you into it.

Often it's peer pressure, stops lads from leaving their mates, even if they don't want to offend.

I was in a group and I was easily influenced. What everyone was doing I was doing'

I was in the wrong crowd. I had plenty of friends and then I started going with friends from when I was younger. Then crime began.

I got mixed up with older people and went off the rails a bit. It depends on the company you're with.

I was with mates who were older than me and we were out nicking every night.

What emerges is the vulnerability of the young person who has to rely on peers, in a group or gang, for their support, their status and their protection as well as for their fun and entertainment. It requires a great deal of self-esteem and confidence to walk away from the crowd especially when, as one young man said, 'they're the only friends you've got'.

For young people who cannot rely on their family for the support and protection that they need there is a particular vulnerability. These are young men without the comforts of their own bedroom in which they can watch TV or play on a personal computer. These are not the boys who will be sitting down for a meal and a talk with their parents. These are the boys who take to the streets for their entertainment and for their friendships and support

Most people, children or adults, are likely to seek out like-minded people and to socialise with them. Groups of people with similar interests and concerns will offer each other support, reassurance and probably some enjoyable activity. One of the reasons that the concept of the self-help group is so successful is that the support provided is through other people who have had a very similar experience and will be able to empathise with a worry or concern. Such groups have entirely positive motivations though there are some that can tip over into more anti-social activity. The rugby team on tour is likely to be drunk and loud at the very least. While none of these groups remotely constitute gangs, some of the reasons for becoming a gang member might be very similar.

The Street Weapons Commission Report (2008) commented that research shows that the children and young people most at risk of gang involvement are those who live in multiply disadvantaged neighbourhoods. The report links structural unemployment and family poverty, exacerbated by negative experiences in school and confrontations with the police and association with gangs. Of course there have been concerns over many years about groups of young people on the streets. What, after all, were Shakespeare's Montagues and Capulets but rival families who jeered at each other and, ultimately, killed each other? Moral panics (Cohen 1972) have arisen over Teddy Boys, Mods and Rockers, Punks and Hells Angels and it is probably true that some of their activities, certainly the violence, might take them closer to the concept of a gang but as the Street Weapons Commission found:

It is not clear that there is a shared and consistent understanding or interpretation of what constitutes a gang and what makes certain types of behaviour 'gang related'. For example, some police forces have used a very broad definition of gang activities, which ranges from congregating in a group, smoking cannabis, drinking to anti-social behaviour and criminal activities.

It is, therefore, difficult to pinpoint who exactly falls within the official definitions of 'gang member'. Gang membership can be taken to include a wide range of people, along an increasing scale of involvement and association. Topped by a minority of older youths (usually taken to mean over 18-years-old) who take part in serious and organized crime to very young 'hangers on' and school children 'running errands' for older offenders with various degrees of regularity. More recent work has also identified other young people who may be rather more 'reluctant' gang members, bullied or coerced into illegal activity.

It is important to bear this fluidity and breadth of definitions in mind when considering official estimates in relation to gang membership and activities. For example, conflating groups of young people who just hang out together in a neighbourhood under the term 'gang' is likely to have an inflationary and alarmist effect on popular and political debate. Various commentators have cautioned against the 'over definition' of youth peer groups as 'gangs' and the 'street socialisation' activities of young people as 'gang activities'.

Two young men tried to describe how and why they got involved in a gang.

Where I lived everyone was in a gang. Even young kids knew about the gang and wanted to be in it because that was where the bigger kids were. If you were part of the gang you had mates who would look after you. You wouldn't ever get bullied because kids would just know that there were bigger kids who would take them on. We had some laughs and some of the stuff was exciting. There was some fighting but I was alright because the big boys would look after me.

There was never any choice really. You had to be part of it or there would be people who would get you. My brothers and all my mates were involved. I didn't have any other friends. And anyway they said you come with us or else and I

43

wasn't going to be the only one in the place that said I wasn't gonna get involved
in it all. Once you're in it's hard to get out. I only ever had a chance to get out
because I got arrested and after I did my time I went to live somewhere else.

Fear of violence, of becoming a victim was also a strong reason for being
part of a gang. Darren was looking to his gang for protection.

Where I was there was a gang that reckoned that this street was their territory.
You couldn't go there. If you went near they might do you. I was alright because
I had my own gang, my own mates who would look after me.

One young man was quite clear that he had only become involved in
a gang because he liked the violence. He was part of a group that used to
orchestrate violence and for him it brought excitement and power. When
he did try to get away from the gang, as he grew older, there was a lot of
pressure to stay involved.

It's hard to get away from it where I live. Everyone is part of a gang and they
know you, and I know them.

For many young men the gang brings many of the things that most of
us would like. Fun and excitement, status, opportunity and power but also
the protection and support that many young people would get from their
parents and their family.

Theories suggest that the family is an all important factor. Farrington
(1996) describes a number of risk factors relating to the family, which may
predict future offending. He suggests that even before birth risk factors
arise. The age and capability of the mother is relevant as is any addiction
to drugs or alcohol during pregnancy. Farrington also comments on the
inter-relationships of these factors with other elements of the home environment, citing research in Newcastle (Kolvin et al, 1988) which found that
neonatal injuries predicted offending up to the age of 32 but only for boys
being raised in deprived families at the age of five. There are many studies that link offending with parental supervision. Wilson (1980) concluded
that lax parenting at the age of ten was linked to future offending. Physical

punishment between the ages of seven and eleven predicted later convictions (Newson and Newson 1989). In the Cambridge Study (Farrington and West 1973) harsh or erratic parental discipline, cruel, passive or neglecting parental attitude, poor supervision and parental conflict all predicted later convictions. The study also found that harsh discipline was a predictor of violent offending.

In 2007 Victim Support published a report linking violent victimisation and offending by young people. There has been some evidence that a broken home and parental separation may also be a predictor but this is more contentious as life with a loving single parent may compensate. However there is some evidence that the presence of a step-parent may lead to friction and there are certainly many comments from young offenders themselves about hostile and sometimes violent relationships with step-fathers which have led to them leaving home, and often sleeping rough, in their early teens.

Research has also pointed to risk factors in homes where there are other criminal members of the family. None of this is surprising. The family is the first human contact that most people will know. It must make a difference if that contact is loving and supportive on the one hand or abusive and violent on the other. One of the long term problems is that the child brought up by violent and abusive parents is far less likely to be able to provide effective parenting for his or her own children.

Problems in a family have far reaching effects. Lack of preparation for school may lead to poor behaviour and conflict in school. Unsupportive or aggressive parents may make it more likely that the child is excluded from school. On every level a child needs a supportive and loving family but many young offenders are not only talking about a lack of parental support they are talking about a family background littered with violence and abuse. Andrew spoke of problems once his mother was in a new relationship:

> Problems at home. My step-dad. I left home, went homeless. I didn't like my step-dad, he didn't like me. It seemed best. That's when a lot of things went wrong.

> I truanted from school just because of problems at home. In the end, in the fifth year, I was excluded. I got sent away during that time; was in and out of

children's homes. There was so much trouble at home. I got a letter saying I was excluded on the day I would have left anyway. It was problems at home put me off it. First few years were brilliant. Got loads of merits. Then home put me off it. Everything went wrong at about fourteen and a half.

Daniel's comments illustrate only too well the impact that a problematic home life can have on other aspects of a young person's life.

Martin did not go into details about the nature of the family problems but it emerged that he had been in and out of care for most of his life

There were a lot of problems. Family problems. I was in care quite a lot.

Noel was much more specific:

I was so afraid of my step-father that I kept a knife under my pillow. I thought my mother would be hurt if she defended me.

Warren and Coleman had both been beaten by one or other of their parents.

My father beat me when I lived with him.

My mother, when I done something bad, she didn't actually beat me up. She used to hit me when I did something wrong like you won't do it again.

David explained why he thought young people got into trouble:

Kids want attention because they have been isolated and abused as a child or because they have no home and friends so they steal from people or shops because they feel as if nobody cares.

His comments are entirely supported by the feelings and experiences described by James, Esco and Tony:

I got passed round the care system. Made me feel unwanted and made me violent to other people.

They just kept moving me around different places, boarding schools, foster parents, homes. I hated it. That's why I used to go round nicking cars and bugger off.

I was put in foster care and then I said I didn't want to stay there and they didn't have anywhere else for me to go so I had to go back there. So I told the social worker where to go and they just turned round and said I wasn't in their care any more, back in the care of my mother and my mother didn't want me so I ended up staying round my friends.

It was because of experiences such as these that Warren thought young people got involved in crime:

Being brought up the wrong way. You think it's the right way till someone tells you different. Need to look at background.

One of the comments made in a Nacro report highlights the compounding of problems when there is no stable home to rely on:

Problems at home led me to hang around street corners as it were. I got into drugs, I didn't have any money so I started stealing then I got into harder, you know higher up the scale like car theft, things like that. Basically if I'd got on with me mum, then a lot of problems that sort of sprouted from that...it's like the seed if you like, drop the seed and the seed was sown when I was kicked out, you know I was kicked out at eleven and that was like the beginning of the problems (Wasted Lives, 1998).

Naz, Jason and Chris had experienced home lives that were a long way from stable and loving, with Chris describing both physical and sexual abuse.

Home was bad. I ran away and lived at the airport for three months. Then I got put in care. I was sleeping rough and I got into drugs. Still angry at my mum and dad.

He used to beat me. Still scars on me back, like whip marks. I don't remember why he did it. Just happened.

Me mam and dad they didn't live together. I was mostly with me mam but I did go to stay with him. But then he started beating me up and his brother tried it on with me. I was only 15. Didn't want any of that and I wouldn't stay there any more.

Some young offenders spoke of levels of violence in the home, where beatings and abuse were very much the norm. On the whole they were not using this as an excuse for becoming involved in crime but were simply explaining that this was the way that it was.

[Dad] never smacked me when I was little 'cause I had an older brother and he got adopted when I was about, when I were about one or something like that, he got adopted because mum, mum had post-natal depression or something like that, she had not long had him, she was smacking him and that when he were crying and stuff like that and she got took off him, so my mum and dad never hit me 'cause they didn't want that to happen to me. When I was older I had a fight with him one time and he knocked me out ... started having a fight, started swearing at him, he said don't you swear at me, I said I'll swear as much as I want at you, he went to hit me like that moved out of the way and I punched him and I thought no what am I doing, what am I doing like that, he started hitting me and that just knocked me out. (Wasted Lives, 1998)

Another participant in the research for the 'Wasted Lives' report described a life history of almost constant violence:

I call him my dad because he's been with me since I was two and I don't know any better. His sister jumped off some flats and killed herself so he's gone on to drink now but me mum's not with him any more 'cause he started beating her up and beating me and my brother Keith up. So it's only since then that I started robbing. I don't think it's got nothing to do with it just ... He used to beat us up with one of them (carpet rods) so. It was only when I was 12 that me and me brother Keith planned to get him. He came in the bedroom and dragged me off the top bunk because me and me brother Keith shared a room, took me off the top bunk by me ankle, and I hit him and he was drunk anyway, he went on the floor and me brother Keith beat him up with the chair. I had to do that to stop him doing it to us. I've grown up with violence all around.

Family problems also contributed to problems in school. Several young offenders accepted that their behaviour had been out of line. For example, Paul acknowledged,

I was very disruptive, anti-authority.

I rebel against authority. Out of spite I would do nothing.

But there were also many examples of the home environment itself as an influence on behaviour in school. Joe, Ben and Charlie all felt that their problems in school had originated with problems at home.

From an early age I had family problems. Life was very up and down. Moved about all over London. Been to 12 schools.

School didn't do anything for me. I just kept not going. I was having a bad time arguing with my mum and dad.

I truanted because of problems at home … step-father.

There were also examples of the family lifestyle making it more difficult to engage in school, as in the case of the young man who said

Only went for a while, from a travelling family.

Non-attendance was an issue for most of the young offenders interviewed. The majority had truanted to a significant extent. Most said that this was because school was boring but there were other factors. Shamon said that he had.

Truanted towards the end. Just lost interest. I got in a bad crowd. Went off the rails.

Wayne just found it more interesting to be out and about or staying at a friend's house than to be in school.

Used to truant for the excitement. Used to walk up and down the streets with friends or go to a friend's house. Got excluded for the amount of trouble I'd been in, not for a specific thing but for the amount.

Simon had lost interest in attending school but it also appeared that his behaviour when he was there was problematic.

After 13 I didn't bother going. I got excluded a couple of times for a couple of weeks then I stopped going. They sent us to a different school. Got taken there in a taxi. I still didn't go, just went out the other door. Then I went to jail at 15.

Robin had started to get into trouble outside of school before his school attendance became sporadic. He was one of many young offenders interviewed who had left school before the official leaving age.

I only started missing school when I went to court. Was excluded for one week for fighting and then I left at 14, no qualifications'.

For John the attraction of a game of football was greater than anything school could offer.

Truanted occasionally. Mostly to play football.

For Leon, however, the alternative attraction was potentially more serious and dangerous.

Truanted a lot towards the end. Got bored, got older. Drugs as well. I was seen as the bully. At first I was a victim but I did a lot of bullying towards the end.

Neil had problems relating to the teachers, though he did not seem to have any difficulty in doing the work.

> I truanted. They weren't teaching me nothing. I was ahead of my year. The teachers would get on my case and I'd get on theirs. Sometimes I'd walk out'.

Kevin, on the other hand found it difficult to cope in the school environment, both because he found the work hard and because his behaviour was volatile.

> I truanted. Found it hard. Stopped going. Other people found it easy. I hung around with people who don't study. I've got a short temper. Get violent. Can't stop.

James and Jason both suggest that they started to truant because that was what everyone else was doing, rather than because of any specific incident or reason.

> Truanted. Everyone did. Couldn't be bothered to go to lessons. Just stopped going.

> Truanting was just something to do-like a fashion.

Crime as an alternative proved to be a more exciting option and as one young man pointed out it had significant material benefits too. For those who had begun to dabble in drugs crime was an apparently obvious way to finance a growing habit. Amil explained,

> Truanted because of the teachers. Teachers with no sense of humour. Got bored. And we were like life is too short. Let's do things. We'd do these robberies and then stay in hotels, drink champagne.

Mark said:,

Didn't go much. I got mixed up in drugs and didn't bother going from about 15. So I did truant but I never got excluded I just left.

One of the factors identified in the literature as having an impact on progress in school is the use of language. Very few of the young offenders contributing to this book were at all articulate. Their language was limited, often crude and showed little sign of social skills. There has been increasing concern that boys have less ability with language than girls. This reflects a concern about the development of literacy skills but also reflects anxiety that the unsophisticated language of young men, particularly working class young men, is insufficient to cope with abstract thought and more mature reasoning.

In 1971 Kelmer-Pringle drew attention to retardation in linguistic ability among children brought up in an institution. The lack of language development also affected reading ability and she found links with aggressive behaviour among poor readers. She concluded that limitations on language development are more of an issue than intelligence or reading attainment. This is a view supported by Head in 1999. He argued that an impoverished command of language inhibits sophisticated thinking. He conceded that the concept of a restricted language code, developed by Bernstein in 1962 is overly simplistic but argued that language is the tool with which we think. Without the capacity for abstract thought there is less chance that a young man will think through the consequences of his actions and the impact they may have on others. Evidence (Farrington, 1996) suggests that young offenders do less well in verbal intelligence tests and prefer to deal with concrete rather than abstract concepts. This lack of skill would also impact on the ability to learn. Of the young men interviewed only a few spoke with any degree of fluency. It may be that this contributed to being seen as 'tough' and 'hard', with bad language and gruff speech contributing to the image as Parker suggested in 1974. However, sentences were short and the style clipped and uncompromising. Few used any sort of linking words. For example,

I had to grow up. I was with my elder brother a lot. People say I'm mature. Can talk like an adult. I see life differently.

This use of language does not reflect a reluctance to talk but rather a limited use of language. This did not stop any of the young men from explaining what they thought but it lacked the more sophisticated use of language, which offers the power to persuade and to disarm the listener. This may be a significant factor in determining who gets excluded from school, who gets arrested, who gets charged. Chambliss' saints would have had the language skills to charm and talk their way out of conflict.

The use of a limited language may also be common to adolescent boys more generally. It is a style of speaking that shows no weakness and demonstrated that the speaker is 'hard' as Parker (1974) suggested. Askew and Ross (1988) point out that young male aggression is demonstrated in many ways. Boys tend to play fight, to be challenging of each other and to take up a tough pose. They suggest that boys fear to show weakness and so there is real pressure to act tough at all times. The fear that if they fail to conform they will be excluded and humiliated offers an explanation for the power of peer pressure.

For some there were problems in school because of their own levels of ability. It has been recognised that a significant number of young offenders have poor literacy skills. This may be because they did not attend sufficiently to learn the basic skills but also because they genuinely could not keep up. Michael had clearly struggled to cope and did not appear to have any additional support to enable him to do so.

> I didn't like school. It was frustrating. They used to put things on the board and then rub it off before I'd finished. Then I wouldn't know what to do.

Ben described himself as having real problems with numbers. He said he was dyslexic with numbers.

> The teacher used to pull me out in front of the class and make me do times tables. I felt humiliated and it made me feel bad at the time.

Louis commented that the worst subjects were those with lots of handwriting.

Loads of handwriting. I found it difficult. I wrote slower than the rest. I was always behind and used to run away. The teachers just gave up.

These comments very much support Hirschi's argument that the child who is not academically able is unlikely to be much enamoured of the school environment.

Problems were not always because of lack of ability. Devlin (1998) commented on the number of prisoners who had struggled in school because they could not see properly or hear sufficiently. One of her examples was Colin who said,

I'm deaf in one ear and going deaf in the other. I had problems with my hearing at school, but I don't know when it started. The classroom was large and I had to learn to lip-read virtually from the start. I did this naturally because my hearing problem wasn't discovered till I got to jail.

Research has also identified a high degree of undiagnosed dyslexia in the prison population. In another example cited by Devlin, Harry, an older prisoner told her,

I always had problems with my reading and later they found out it was dyslexia, but at the time I was just told I was thick. Till I was eight everybody thought I was just messing around and then they discovered I needed glasses.

Family background is relevant to this. Someone needs to notice that a child does not see as well as others before the child is likely to be aware that they are long or short sighted. Someone has to be talking to the child in order to realise that they can't hear properly. Dysfunctional and neglectful parenting is unlikely to be attentive to these concerns. Even if there is recognition there may be a reluctance to do anything about it in case it involves a cost.

Many young offenders have been excluded from school. Apart from the obvious consequences of limited education and lack of any sort of qualification this was also significant in many cases because it contributed to time on the streets and to boredom. Many of the young men interviewed were philosophical about the fact that they had been excluded. One commented that the teachers could not cope with his behaviour any more. In another example the exclusion resulted from his hitting the head teacher and appreciated the fact that this probably meant that exclusion was inevitable. John was excluded for taking drugs into school and David had burgled the school, again making exclusion pretty inevitable. Julian had been excluded for 'Fighting. Being a pain in the arse'. Clint said that he,

> went to school till [I] was 13. I just messed about, skipping lessons, talking. Wasn't interested. Got excluded for fighting.

He was far from unique in being excluded for violence in some form. Exclusion for fighting was a regular occurrence, especially for those young men who were interviewed while still in prison.

Kahn was one of a small number who had been excluded because of his poor attendance.

> Got excluded for truanting. Had so much time off.

But for most there were examples of fighting and violence involving other pupils and, in some cases, the teaching staff. David had been fighting and misbehaving very early in his school career.

> I went to school but I got excluded from primary school only about a week before I finished there. It was for fighting and being the class clown. I was out of school for a couple of years.

The exclusion came much later for Rob but in the end he was only allowed in school to take his GCSEs.

> I was excluded. They let me do my exams. I got suspended loads of times but they finally said I was excluded. I was excluded about two weeks before the exams. For fighting. I just kept getting into trouble and fighting.

Anwar had eventually faced exclusion because of his violence towards a teacher. There had clearly been problems with relationships with his peers as well as with the staff and it was his dislike of teacher attitudes that meant he did not report alleged bullying:

> Got excluded because I threw a chair at a teacher. He was treating me like a little kid and even a little kid has got rights. Talk to me nicely and I talk to you nicely. I was bullied at school. Not physical. Calling me a Paki, racist stuff. It made me harder. Not physical but in myself. I never told the teachers. I didn't like some of the teacher attitudes, like I'm superior, you've got no say. Even when you know you're right.

Both Cas and Delroy admitted to behaviour that was extreme:

> I didn't always go and got excluded for fighting and violence. Used to be escorted to school. Was banned from some areas by the police.

> I did go to school but got kicked out when I was 14 and never went back. When I was at primary school I went … I can only describe it as a naughty school. Then I went to secondary for 14 months. Expelled for bad behaviour. Too much for the school. I thought school was a place where you could meet other people, other lads and mess around. That's what I thought at the time.

While there was acceptance that their behaviour was difficult and perhaps unacceptable there was also a sense that teachers might have done more to help or to understand the reasons for the bad behaviour. As Julian said,

> I reckon they had a mind-set about how kids should be and I was nothing like that. They wanted kids to be bright yet dumb. Kids that did as they were told. Some of the teachers understood me but very few.

Peter added that there were no second chances, once you had misbehaved you were assumed to behave badly always. As an example he said that he had intervened in a fight to help another pupil. The others involved in the fight were given detention but he was excluded. Jason still felt a strong sense of injustice that his behaviour had been taken at face value, without any apparent thought that there might be reasons for it.

I didn't behave well at school. I got into a lot of trouble and I'm not pretending I was some little angel. But they never asked me if things were okay at home, if there was any reason why I used to get angry. And there was trouble at home. Both me mum and me dad used to drink. They used to come back from the pub and have these big fights. Wake us all up. It was really hard to get up in the morning when you'd been awake half the night.

Conflict with teachers was often seen as the reason for disliking school. Evan blamed the attitude of teachers even though he accepted that his behaviour might have been less than perfect.

Teachers. They was no help. Used to have arguments with the teachers but that was probably because I was young.

Conflict with other pupils is also an issue. Rutter, Giller and Hagel (1998) have suggested that young offenders at the more serious end of the spectrum often have difficulty in relationships with peers as well as with adults. Bullying was seen as part and parcel of school life, though not many would admit to being the victim of bullying. Askew and Ross (1988) have commented that bullying is related to the extent to which physical power is part of the stereotypical male attributes. Bullying is a way in which boys can demonstrate their manliness. If this is the case it is not surprising that boys do not want to admit to a victim status that might diminish their own masculinity.

Bullying was none the less an issue in some cases and with far reaching consequences. John was 17. He had left school at 15 without any qualifications. He had been out of school for the whole period of secondary school and had only attended for about a year. This was because he did not like the atmosphere.

There was too much bullying and violence.

Some of the alleged bullying was from teachers.

Even had a fight with one teacher. He picked me up and threw me across the room so I hit him on the chin and kicked his leg.

He was bullied by other pupils too.

> Near enough everyone in the year above me [so that the worst thing about school was] every day walking in through the gates knowing something's going to happen.

For James bullying had tragic consequences. He was 20 and serving a life sentence for manslaughter. There had been some bullying and he had taken a knife into school. He said that he had been bullied.

> An awful lot. There was years of bullying and I bottled it up and it came out the wrong way. I have Aspergers syndrome. It's a form of autism. I didn't mix with the others and I stood out from the rest. Got picked on'.

He had some ability and had enjoyed many of his lessons but his teachers did not take his complaints of bullying seriously, even though his parents had visited the school to complain. Bullying,

> ...made me aggressive to deal with it. Looking back I can see that I did have some good times but I look back and see some awful memories.

By the age of 13 he was in a secure unit.

Other victims of bullying became the bullies themselves. They learned to fight back. Peter said he had been a bully because

> Kids would start on me and I can't back down. I was a bit podgy at school so some kids said things. I hit them.

The influence of friends in school was critical for many young offenders. The wrong friends had led to truancy and ultimately to involvement in crime but some conceded that they had had some choice in this. Joe had been a sociable young man and his comments demonstrate that it is possible to choose the friends who will be working and those that will not.

I could fit in with the good side and the bad side. If I wanted to work I'd go with the ones who wanted to work and when I didn't I'd sit with the bad boys. When it really counted I spent too much time with the bad boys.

Seeking out the 'bad boys' or being the one who took things too far was sometimes the case. Desmond took things a step further than his friends.

A lot got their heads down and stayed on to the sixth form. There were a couple like me who dropped out early and they're in prison now. Sad but that's the way it is.

Cas described a disrupted schooling, which was partly because of family problems. He said that he had problems with authority and that he only worked for the teachers who were nice to him. He made friends easily, even though he attended a lot of different schools. Most of those friends did not like school but their behaviour was never as extreme as his own.

I made friends easily. They didn't like school either. They found me funny. I took thing to the limit when others didn't. Some said I was a joker.

It is easy enough to imagine that a boy who comes late into a school should make friends by being 'the class clown' and providing entertainment for others through his disruptive behaviour. There also seems to be an issue about knowing when to stop. Young offenders spoke often about friends who had also misbehaved in and out of school but who had settled down and gone on to college or employment. Lee was in prison and said of his school friend, 'They used to be the same as me but they've all got jobs now'.

Rob was very much aware that he had wasted a lot of opportunities:

I went to school till I was 14 or 15 then I started tossing off. I was knocking about with older people. I really regret it now. I just messed around all the time so the teachers knew I did and had no time for me. Wish I'd stuck it out. Probably could have done something at school if I wasn't being so mad. Could have stayed on for A levels but I didn't do. A lot of mates stick it out. Some did like me but the majority did well at school. They're okay now. Got cars and that and I'm still walking.

The relationship with teachers was, for many, a critical factor in whether they could make a go of school or whether they either dropped out or were thrown out. This is hardly surprising. A teacher is the first real authority figure that most children meet outside the home and it is, therefore, inevitable, that they will have an impact on their pupils' lives. A good teacher could make the subject interesting and motivate the student but for these young offenders this seems to have happened all too rarely. Confrontation seems to have been a regular occurrence for many young offenders. For the most part there is also acknowledgement that it was their own disruptive behaviour that provoked negative responses from teachers but there were also comments that suggested some very poor classroom management on the part of the teacher. One suggestion was that this was because of a dislike of boys:

> They would talk to the girls. They were alright with the girls but the boys it was always just get on with your work. Just telling us what to do.

There was some suggestion that a dislike of an individual stemmed from a dislike of older brothers or sisters. Ian said,

> Couldn't get on with the teachers. My sister went to the school and they hated her and must have thought I'd be the same. My little brother gets it now and he's brainier than me.

Steve said,

> Never liked school and the teachers hated me so it wasn't worth going. My brother was just leaving when I started. They hated him and passed it on to me. My sister too. My mum used to have to take her to school to stop her bunking off. She used to go in the front door and out the back'

There was also some element of living down to teacher expectations. Mark said,

My brother went to the same school as me. He was older. He was a pain in the arse at school. Got into loads of trouble. When I went there the first thing they said was 'I suppose you'll be just like your brother'.

There also seems to have been a stereotyping of pupils from particular areas Jes said that

...the worst thing about school was the way the teachers used to treat us. I come from a rough area and everyone from that area had a bad time.

Pete was lucky in that an alternative was found but he had also experienced stereotyping.

The school I went to you couldn't learn in. One the teachers had pictured you then you were bad. Then I went to a college project. It was a place for people who got kicked out of school but you were in the same classes with everyone else. You could do any course. I did business studies.

Looking back on school days many of the young men regretted their behaviour or at least the consequences of it. Ross explained,

Now I think school was the best time of my life. Then I hated it. I used to get to the gate, turn round and go back to bed when me mam was out.

Or as Jim put it,

I truanted. School didn't interest me. Left at 16 but I never took exams. I wish I was there now. I could have got some qualifications and a job.

Or David,

When I was at school I didn't like it. Regret it now I think. I got excluded from a good school. Then I went to a bad school and got excluded in the third year for fighting and messing around.

Barry had enjoyed some aspects of school. He had enjoyed learning new things but had only worked at the things he liked doing.

> Best thing about school? Learning innit? Having the buzz what you had. Every day something new and a good buzz. But I was only learning what I wanted to learn and two fingers to anything I didn't like.

His friend Sy, however, had not liked any of it. Looking back he admitted he had been foolish, especially in just walking out for no particular reason.

> I hated school. I just left. Don't know why. Trouble. Stupid things. Every day I woke up thinking truanting. I was stupid when I was young.

Whether because of learning difficulties or because of behavioural problems some young offenders have received education in special units or through home tuition. The options were not always a success. Certainly not for Danny who said,

> Early on I went to school. Other than normal school I did a special school and then boarding school. Expelled for fighting. I was always getting chucked out for fighting. It wasn't always my fault. I went to boarding school and left after a day. I beat up two kids before lunch. The headmaster said why and I said it was because I didn't want to be at the school. He said you only had to tell me. I would fight anybody. I was a bully.

James also had difficulties.

> I got excluded for messing about in class. I got suspended a few times. I was excluded from primary school and went to a special school. Then I went to a special secondary school. I did alright there and got sent back to secondary school and I got expelled. Went back to special school again. It was out of my area. When I was at home I used to fight and that.

After being out of school for two years John went to a special school, which he described as a last resort school. He was bullied there by the older boys and found it difficult to keep up with the work. Gary had a private tutor after he was excluded from school for possession of cannabis. Looking back he realised that his own bad attitude had caused him problems but at the time he was not even prepared to work on a one to one basis with the tutor and he gave up on that.

Peter was more positive about home tuition:

> I had a private tutor. Me mum took me out of school because I was getting in too many fights. I was a bully. That's why I had to leave. I didn't mean to but kids would start on me and I can't back down. I hated school. Everything I hated. Tuition it was alright. I didn't listen to what they said about qualifications. I just thought they were trying to make me work harder.

Matthew had truanted from mainstream school.

> I did go but not much. I got kicked out and went to a unit. I got kicked out of there and went to another unit. I just deteriorated and didn't go. Faded away.

Talking to young offenders a few years after they left school most show a high level of awareness that their behaviour was out of order. Although for some there were family problems which made it harder to cope in school, it would be wrong to think that it was always because their parents did not try to ensure that they had a decent education.

Paul said,

> I went to school but I was excluded in the second year. Then I went to a private school that my mum sorted out. I didn't truant. My mum was strict. If it hadn't been for her I wouldn't have gone so much. I was excluded for being a prat. You don't think school is important when you're young. You just think it's a laugh with your mates. When you get older you think different.

Strict parents who insisted on school attendance often made the difference between turning up and truancy. Sean said,

> Me Mam was always on the case.

Matthew, John and Phil had all had parents, or at least one parent who insisted that they attend school and made sure that they did.

> Didn't miss school, well now and then, but my mum was strict.

> Didn't truant, down to my parents more than anything.

> I went to school because I was told. My parents said go.

Dealing with school attendance and behaviour in school was not always easy for the family. Joe said,

> My mum used to take me to school to make sure I got there. I just used to go out the back door and go home after she'd gone to work.

While Paul remembered,

> I was suspended once for running up a corridor and I bumped into a teacher. I was out for a week. I couldn't go back till mum went in and I didn't tell her for a week.

David used to be excluded regularly for fighting.

> I used to be off two weeks every time. I used to be off till they'd seen my mum and that's how I used to get the two weeks. Then they threw me out.

Some parents, although caring and wanting to offer support, are just not able to do it. At a family intervention project run by Nacro a key worker was asked to visit the mother of three children who had started to truant from school and to behave badly when they did attend. The mother had been the victim of domestic violence and was still afraid that her husband would find her again. She spoke very little English and had been shunned by her family because she had left her husband. She was unsupported and isolated, increasingly troubled by debt and becoming chronically depressed. She simply could not cope with her children and was unable to offer the support and stability that they needed. Working with the mother to provide her with help and support meant that she was again able to provide the parenting support that the children needed. Within a relatively short time their school attendance and general behaviour had improved dramatically. Recognition that parents may need support, not only with managing a new baby but also in dealing with the management of growing children may be an important step in reducing the number of children excluded from school or of becoming involved in crime.

It is also the case that a disproportionate number of young offenders have experienced bereavement. One young man explained that he now lived with his sister because his mother had died. Apart from the obvious trauma of losing a parent at a young age there is the additional possibility that there will not be someone who makes sure that the child is up and ready for school, or who is prepared to visit the school if there are problems. Pete explained that his father had not been able to cope after the death of his wife:

> He went to pieces really. He drank a lot more than he used to and he didn't really know what to do to look after us. My mum had always done all that. She was the one who used to get us sorted for school and all that.

Dave's mother had been the peacemaker in an all male household. When she was no longer present, there were more fights and arguments between the three boys in the family and their father.

> When my mum died and it was just my dad and me and my brothers we did have a lot of fights. She was always the one who sort of calmed us down before.

And, far from providing support, there will be families who make matters far worse. Wayne spoke about what happened when he was excluded for three days for fighting.

> Me dad went up the school and said he wanted to see the teacher. He lost his rag and started shouting and carrying on. They had to call the police in the end. They said that they wouldn't have him back in the school and that's when they said they would chuck me out for good and all.

There are some obvious consequences of failure and exclusion in school. Many offenders have left school before the school leaving age; some because they have been excluded and some because they chose to walk out. As Gavin explained,

> I found school really boring. I just walked out. I was having an argument with the art teacher and I just said 'kiss my arse' and walked out…

The result is a lack of any formal qualification, which, in turn, makes it far harder to find work. Even if it is possible to find employment it is likely to be lower paid and to make it more difficult to find suitable and affordable housing.

This alone makes it more difficult to get a start in life, to live independently and to have status as a responsible adult but the problem may be further compounded as in Gavin's case, where,

> …me mum chucked me out. I've been on the streets since I was 14.

A 14-year-old living on the streets, with no source of legitimate income must be at great risk of getting into crime, if only to provide himself or herself with enough money to eat. The 'Transition to Adulthood' reports draw attention to the fact that the child of middle class and supportive parents is likely to receive support until the or she turns 21. The unsupported child, probably with fewer personal resources seems to be expected to survive and prosper without the same opportunities. This is clearly an unrealistic expectation. If we add into the equation the number of young offenders who have mental health issues and are reliant on drugs and alcohol it becomes even less realistic. Early involvement in crime also becomes a compounding factor. If it was true that at school there was a sense that once you were identified as bad you would always be deemed to be bad how much more true is this of involvement in the criminal justice system. A criminal record closes doors to employment, further education, insurance, credit and seriously reduces the chance of finding somewhere decent to live. John was very worried about his future:

You see I don't know what will happen because of my criminal record and if it's going to affect anything. I don't know if ABH is classed as serious. I like working with kids, take them on activities and that. I don't know—I'll find out when I get out. It'll probably be a dead end and I'll have to go and find something else to do.

The result is a particularly vicious spiral. No job means no money and 'if you have no money it is easy to steal'. Not enough money to pay rent leads to sofa surfing and rough sleeping and then 'you are back with the old mates and the old games'. How do you find work when you have no place to live? What do you do when there is nowhere to get washed or wash your clothes? How can you go to a job interview when all you have are a few grubby clothes? How can you focus on looking for work when you have no idea where you will sleep tonight?

The system makes it easy to believe that it is 'once a criminal always a criminal'. The fact of a criminal record makes everything harder; except perhaps further crime. Once in the system it is very hard indeed to get out again. Lee was not alone in voicing desperation.

Can't read or write. Got a criminal record. What the fuck are you going to do? You start robbing and robbing. From robbing you start selling drugs. Some went straight to rob banks and got some bad sentences and some started killing people. It's total sadness.

So it is a gloomy picture for a young man, easy to feel that it is already too late. And it is very hard to break long term habits as any former smoker would attest. It is especially difficult if you are trying to make a big change in lifestyle without resources, help or support.

And yet, in the end, most young offenders do break the habit, make the change. They do stop offending. Why?

CHAPTER THREE

IMMATURITY AND GROWING UP

If he has a conscience he will suffer for his mistake.
That will be punishment as well as the prison.
Fydor Dostoevsky, *Crime and Punishment*, Chapter19.

To some extent there will always be an element of mystery about why most young offenders, some of them prolific offenders, stop offending as they get older. There is equally an element of mystery about the extent to which it simply happens so that they gradually desist from offending and the extent to which they stop because of either fear of punishment or through effective rehabilitation. Possibly unhelpfully, it is often suggested that it is when the right thing happens to the right person at the right time but this has an element of truth. Offenders stop offending if they want to and if the circumstances are such as to allow them to stop.

Paul tried to explain how he reached the point where he was just not involved in crime any more. For him it was a combination of recognising that what he was doing was wrong and having something else in his life to care about.

> I think I did know before that what I was doing was not right. I was just mental
> then though, never really thought about what I was doing. I got a job so I didn't
> need the money and I was living with me missis so I had a good place to live and
> I didn't want to lose it and I just started to think about it and thought 'this is just
> fucking stupid'. I just stopped going out drinking with the usual crowd and I just
> never got into trouble after that.

There is considerable literature to support the view that, gradually, young men stop offending. Matza (1964) described the notion of drift. They drift into crime and they drift out of it again. Rutherford (1995) describes a process of growing out of crime while Nettler (1974) said that they 'mature out'.

This would certainly be consistent with the concept of troubled adolescence where behaviour is often risky and reckless and there is a search for excitement. That need for risk and adventure appears to diminish with age, possibly because a more mature adult does have a better sense of consequence. In 1986 Farrington identified the peak age of offending as 16-20 and in 1978 Blumstein, Cohen and Nagin had commented that most offenders have stopped offending by the time they are 28.

For many young people, whether offenders or not, the period between 20 and 28 is likely to be a period of change and transition. This is a time when they might get a job, develop a long term relationship with a partner, become a parent, move into their own accommodation. All of these will change the perspective on responsibility and on having something to lose.

Mark was clear about what had made a difference for him.

> What made a big difference was getting a decent place to stay. Once you've got something halfway decent you don't want to muck up and lose it.

Maruna (2000) identifies three broad theoretical perspectives. Maturational reform theories have been prevalent for many years and relate to the link between age and some criminal activity. Social bond theories suggest that it is the ties to family, employment or education as young people grow towards adulthood. Essentially these ties mean that they have something to lose which they would not want to lose. The third set of theories, narrative theories relate more to personal change in the sense of self and identity, which leads to greater thought for other people and greater awareness of possible consequences.

Paul's experience suggests a combination of all these factors. He was becoming aware as he grew older that his behaviour was not right and he also now had something to lose. He was in a relationship and had a decent place to live.

Theory does not support the view that any old job or any old relationship will make the difference. Sampson and Laub (1993) stressed the importance of the quality of these bonds while Crutchfield (1995) stated that a low level job was unlikely to reduce involvement in crime. Similarly a marriage or long term partnership with another person involved in crime is unlikely to result in desistance. Research in Finland suggested that becoming a parent contributes to desistance but this may be because there is a good level of support for the young parent. In the USA, Wakefield and Uggen (2008) pointed to a risk of further offending because of the increase in hardship. This was very much reflected in a comment that Jim made:

> I didn't want to get into any more trouble because we had the bairn and I really didn't want to go inside again and not see him. It was dead hard though. So much stuff you have to have with a kid. She couldn't work cos of looking after him and I couldn't get a decent job. I just needed some money so much.

In a 2010 report, Theobald and Farrington suggest that it is early marriage which may have a greater impact on offending. Men who married later tended more often to maintain something of their former lifestyle and their wives appeared to have less influence on them. They further suggest that desistance may not depend so much on getting married but on the investment in a long term relationship.

Joe would agree:

> I had been going out with my girlfriend for a long time but it was always a bit on and a bit off. Especially when I got into any trouble. Then, about a year ago I thought that it was all getting stupid. I wanted to be with her. I wanted that more than I wanted to be pissing about with my mates. We got a place and there you go. Happy ever after. At least I hope so.

There has always been a suggestion, supported by several research studies, that having a job, a relationship, stability and regular income will all contribute to desistance. Even so Sampson and Laub (1993) have strongly suggested that desistance is rarely a deliberate and orderly process. There may be examples of Road to Damascus conversions but for most people it is likely to be a long, and not very steady process. Arguably it is never possible to know whether someone has completely desisted from offending until they are dead. It is always possible that someone who has not committed an offence for years might suddenly become involved in crime again. This is relatively unusual. What is more likely is that there will be a gradual change

71

in lifestyle so that offending becomes less serious and or less frequent until eventually it ceases to be part of the lifestyle at all.

For many young men it is likely that the gradual process will occur alongside subtle changes in their environment. Gangs and groups break up as either members move away, find partners and settle down or because leaders are arrested and imprisoned. Partners object to criminal friends and for some there will be a choice between the activities of the old crowd and the demands of a new family. Farrington and West's longitudinal study appeared to suggest that getting married and moving out of London were of special significance.

Grant speculated on where things had changed and how the group had broken up, making it possible for him to pull away from the group culture.

> Why did I stop getting into trouble? Don't know really. I used to be with a crowd and then they started sort of drifting off. One bloke got married and then he never came out. A couple of them got nicked and they got long sentences. Bit of a warning to the rest of us maybe. But I didn't like say I am not going to do crime any more. It sort of happened and I haven't been in trouble for a long time.

None of this has much to do with the criminal justice system, punishment or rehabilitation but young offenders themselves did not rule out the possibility that punishment, or the fear of it, might be the trigger to stop offending.

Dave thought people stopped because 'they don't want to get sent down' and Pete similarly said it was because 'they don't want to go to jail'. John thought it was

> ...because they're scared of the prisons or going back to prison for a sentence to be finished.

Joe suggested that,

> The consequences of robbing [would influence people and they would want to] stop going to jail.

David said that he thought it was because

…they realise it's not worth the hassle of being punished.

Certainly Alex, who had a string of convictions by the end of his teens, was very aware that the next custodial sentence would be in an adult prison and the prospect of that worried him far more that the prospect of another stretch in a young offender institution.

Punishment, research tells us, only works if certain conditions are fulfilled. It must be inevitable, immediate, comprehensible and the person punished must be able to behave differently (McGuire 2002). Punishment through the criminal justice system does not always meet these conditions. It is not inevitable. The offender must be caught and convicted and that will not always be the case. It is not usually that immediate. A more serious charge, especially if there is a not guilty plea, may take months to come to court. Not all punishments are comprehensible. Anti-social behaviour orders (ASBOs) and licence requirements (on release or leave from custody) can be so complicated and extensive that the offender is unclear what is required. Darren had been the subject of an ASBO.

> It was just a nightmare. There were all these conditions. I couldn't go to this place. I couldn't spend time with me mates. I had to keep reporting in. It was just too much. Couldn't remember half what I was supposed to do.'

And the person punished must be able to behave differently. This is not always possible, at least at the time of the punishment. The offender with mental health issues who has behaved in a particular way because of his or her mental state will not be changed by punishment. The addict who steals to fund a habit is unlikely to stop stealing unless able to kick the habit. Research also tells us that young offenders are likely to have a very poor sense of the consequences of their actions and so are less likely to associate what they do with the prospect of punishments. So punishment alone is not going to be a solution to the problem.

Young offenders, though, did not all subscribe to the research view that it is the acquisition of a home, a job or a partner that is critical to desistance or to rehabilitation. Most suggested that the main reason that people stop is that they have made a personal choice to do so and because they realise that their behaviour has been wrong or foolish. There were several interpretations of this

John thought it was because

They realise it's stupid or that they have gone too far.

While Jack just thought

They sort their lives out.

Musse said, 'They want to change their lifestyle'. He added that this was what he was trying to prepare for after his release. He said,

I've learned a lot. We watch films about AIDS, heroin, life outside. I get books from the library, I get Tintin books, easy to read. Some laugh but I say I can't read a great long book. Pictures, actions help me read. I go to the library every week. Mum will be disappointed if I haven't changed.

Peter said he thought young offenders stopped so that they could 'sort their lives out and change their life around'. Dave also spoke of a desire to 'change their lifestyle'. Some of the young offenders associated the change with growing up. Alan, for example, said 'Some may realise that they are getting nowhere. Some may grow out of it. Not find it fun any more'. Paul said he thought 'They grow up. Think different. Trusting people and settle down'. Ian summed up the process as

Because people eventually realise they are being a dick whether that is before or after prison.

Gary agreed

Because people grow and become more mature and eventually realise that the things they do doesn't get them anywhere.

Lee commented on some of the factors that go with age saying,

Age. Having kids to be an example to. Wanting to lead a normal life.

Other comments supported this concept of wanting to be 'normal' and moving on. One group of young offenders all had much the same comments to make:

Cos they want to.

Because they want to get on with their lives.

Because they want to change.

Because of growing up, realised it's stupid.

They usually give up and take things more seriously.

And, as Damian said,

They realise it's wrong.

Matthew was made aware that his persistent car theft and joy-riding was wrong when he took part in a programme being run during his sentence. The programme contained some graphic images of crashes and the consequences of joy-riding:

They showed us these films and it had loads of stuff about crashes and about people getting hurt. It was all about joy-riding. Made me think I don't want to be doing that. Save up. Buy a bike. Get a job and get on with life.

So there is some consensus among young offenders that there is simply a point when people realise that crime is wrong or at least that it is no longer fun or necessary. McIvor, Jameson and Murray's (1999) study in Scotland found that in the youngest age group desistance was associated with the real and potential consequences of offending and a growing recognition that offending was pointless and wrong. However, both theorists and offenders suggest a very significant proviso.

Maruna and Immarigeon (2004) make it clear that the desistance process is not an easy one nor is it a speedy process. Making a transition from involvement in crime to becoming a responsible adult is not easy and there are difficulties in making that transition, however genuine the desire to change.

Paul accepted the need for punishment but thought that

> Sometimes after they've received punishment they get led on another route.

He suggested that it was what happened after the punishment that could make a difference. Evan also thought that some sort of guidance or help was required.

> They get help and support or something happens that makes them want to change.

Noel was quite clear that change was

> …because they have been given help and support to turn their lives around.

Wanting to change is not at all the same as being able to change and there are many obstacles in the way of change that will lead to delays in the desistance process for many young offenders. Location appears to be important for example. Smith (2006) found that desistance was dependent on the area where the young person lived. Continuing to offend was more common in deprived neighbourhoods and in neighbourhoods that were perceived to be disorderly. One of the reasons that offenders often give for a return to crime is that they have gone back to the area that they came from, often a deprived and/or disorderly one.

> I came out in September and I told them that I couldn't go back to where I was before because that's where all my trouble was. They said I couldn't go anywhere else because I wouldn't have no link with anywhere else, and you have to have lived in the place before. So there I am, back where I bloody started.

For many young offenders there will be specific pressures not to stop offending. Drug dealers certainly won't want people to stop using drugs and will target an individual known to be a potential buyer. Criminal associates will not want a former 'colleague' to stop. They might be needed on another job or they may present a risk that, if they are going straight, they will inform on former associates. It is one of the reasons that some young offenders give for the difficulty in leaving a gang. Sometimes, therefore, the pressures will be deliberate and enforced by sanctions.

> I wanted to stop. I really did want to stop. I didn't want to be in any more trouble and I didn't want to be in a gang no more. But they all knew me and I knew all them. They said they'd fucking kill me if I didn't go with them. They thought I'd grass them up.

Sometimes it will just be that it is the same group of friends who assume that the individual is still part of the crowd and doing the same sort of thing. The latter pressures should be understood by anyone who has tried to give up on the prevailing activity of a group of friends. Trying to give up or even cut down on alcohol use is often difficult for anyone who has a social circle that drinks regularly. Adults comment that they have used excuses such as 'taking antibiotics' to avoid being pressured into drinking. If, generally, responsible adults are resorting to tricks to avoid the pressure from friends how much more difficult will that be for a young person with a limited circle of friends and at an age where the esteem of peers is of immense importance? It takes courage to be the first one to give up on something and that includes walking away from crime.

> When I came out I hadn't been drinking, obviously. I hadn't felt too bad either so I thought now is the time. Keep off the stuff. Me mates came to meet me at the gate. Straight down the pub so we could celebrate me being out. Back to square one I was.

One group of young prisoners speaking about their future plans spoke of marrying, settling down, getting jobs. All fairly normal aspirations for young men. There were two caveats though. The first was that they did not expect to be able to achieve what they wanted because of their criminal record. The second was 'you can say anything while you're still in here'.

They were all too aware that talking about their plans for the future, their intention to stay out of trouble was only too easy, i.e. when they were still in prison. It was only after release that the feasibility of their plans and the strength of their own motivation would be put to the test. Without exception they thought that however much they tried they would still be rejected. For some of them it was too much of a forgone conclusion for them even to try.

One young man had been in custody for a long time. He had been involved with his older brothers in a serious offence so that, although still a young man, he had been inside for several years. He had done all he possibly could to improve his chances on release. He had worked his way through GCSEs and A-levels and had finally achieved a degree. As he planned for his release and came up against some of the obstacles to making a go of it on the outside he commented, 'I might just as well commit another offence. If I get back in here I'll do an MA'. Cynical the view may be but it is a demonstration of the difficulty of facing life after custody.

Even for those who have not experienced prison there are still obstacles to changing a way of life, which may have brought pleasure, excitement and considerable income. On release the realities of the housing shortage and the job market start to kick in and former friends and former dealers will begin to offer all sorts of temptations to go back to the life that was before.

Both Esco and John were still intending to commit crime after release. They both knew that their options for legitimate income would be limited and that they could obtain more money to live on through crime.

> There's no jobs out there. Nothing for me. I can make good money dealing. I can have a good life.

> I'm not stopping crime. I can rob enough to live on. More than I could get from some stupid boring job.

The practicalities are of huge importance. Housing is crucial. Lee was

> Staying in a car. The outreach team used to come and see me.

The return to the same neighbourhood and the same level of housing also presents a daunting prospect. Jim said,

> Perhaps I had false expectations. It is pretty dismal to know that you're going to be re-housed in the same street that you were in before. It seems set up to fail.

Linden was very anxious about his forthcoming release. He knew that he was going back to an environment where he would be vulnerable to involvement in crime and drugs, especially since he had been told that life was harder on the outside now than it had been when he came into jail.

> I really didn't want to go back to my mum and my girlfriend and my little boy and that because of all the drugs and my mates and that. I was speaking to one of my mates and he was saying it has got a lot worse out there and I've been in jail for 15 months so it'll be a lot worse and I'm not looking forward to going out tomorrow really.

Phil saw the possibility of accommodation as almost the be all and end all

> Everything needed is finding somewhere to live.

His point is emphasised by Darren's comments. Darren had been in HM Young Offender Institution Portland and so received help from Nacro's On Side project. He said,

> Been homeless twice. It's so good having a flat. So much relief at having no worries about where to sleep at night.'

Colin, another young man involved with the same project said that his greatest worries were

> ...like not having a place to live and that, you know? And getting back into committing crime ...and not having support and that.

A roof over your head is a pretty basic need for most people, though it needs to be rather more than that if it is going to help someone from slipping back into crime. Dan was coming to the end of his sentence and started to look for somewhere to live on his return to London. He contacted over 40 housing associations but with little success. At the last minute he found a room in a multi-occupancy property. What he found, on his arrival, was that no one else in the building had work, or had any intention of finding work. Some of the tenants were drug users and visits from dealers were commonplace. The lock on his room was faulty and some of his possessions were stolen from the room within a few hours of his moving in. Accommodation needs to be safe and appropriate if it is going to help.

Getting a job is the next priority for many offenders who want to go straight. It is, however, no easy matter to find work, not with a criminal record. Peter said,

> I tried to get a job. Must have done tons of applications. Once they knew I had a record they didn't want to know.

Jim thought that he had found himself work.

> I got a job and then a new manager came and he told me that he didn't want me because I'd got a record.

A perception that rejection by employers would be automatic was a real worry for many of the young men involved in the interviews. This was especially for those who had served a prison sentence.

> I am not sure what to do on release when I go for interview and I am asked about criminal record. If I put down yes I will not get the job.

It is perhaps not so surprising that when the rejections turn out to be real frustration and anger causes some young men to return to crime.

> When I got out of jail I wanted to go legit and get a job and all that but it was very hard because I wasn't getting no help from my probation and I went to

about 60 interviews, like three in a week and I had a lot of certificates which I got in jail like CLAIT and CAD and a lot more so I was well suitable for these jobs but I kept getting turned away because of my robbery conviction which I put on the application form. I didn't fill it in for Royal Mail and I got the job and then got fired after three weeks because they found out which I found humiliating that I was trying to be law-abiding and getting fucked about. I just gave up and went back to what I know—crime.

Repeated failure to find employment, even with some qualifications and skills to offer is a daunting prospect for anyone. Damian was left desperate and anxious.

I went all round trying to get a job. They wouldn't give me the time of day. I know it was my record. And there's kids round here with no record what can't get jobs. Who's going to take me on?

One young man was a little more optimistic. He said,

I feel that with qualification I'll get a job. I've got more confidence. Without them they'd see criminal record and that's that.

Despite the fact that many offenders come from dysfunctional homes and have spent time with criminal friends, several suggested that it was only because of friends or family that they would be able to find any work at all.

Evan thought that his dad would find him work on the building site and Joe thought that his brother might give him a job. James thought he would get work because

…my friend is running his own business so I can go back and work for him. Painting and decorating.

The young offenders who had worked before coming into custody were more hopeful, though still likely to rely on a member of their family.

Dave was fairly confident and said,

> I'm a fork lift truck driver. I'll get my job back. Or my father is a mason and with bricklaying qualifications I could work with him.

Craig thought,

> I might get my job back where I worked before. Dad is a foreman so it should be okay.

Carl had been forced to change his plans but thought that his parents would help him.

> I wanted to be in the army but I've been in over three years so I can't ever have a firearm. They're not likely to take me on. I suppose they might have some things I could do but it would be very limited. Me mum and dad will get me a job.

For most young offenders there was a very clear need for help and support in sorting out practicalities. Many also had a very obvious need for emotional support. For some it was family and friends but not all parents could or would provide it. Richie said,

> Stayed with my parents but we had arguments and I couldn't get out and cool down because of a tag. So much better that I have my own place.

For a great many it was local projects and project staff that provided support, practical and emotional, and the encouragement that had been absent for most of their lives. Comments from a number of young offenders who were benefitting in some way from such support demonstrates the massive difference it has made in their lives. Clive had really appreciated the wide range of help he had received.

> I have only good things to say. I get additional support for my dyslexia. I've had help with my college course and to sort out my council tax. I've been in jail all my life. Now I have the support and I really appreciate it. I think this is a stepping stone and I am now on the path to independence.

One comment from Darren demonstrates the difference that it makes when there are people who do seem to care about you and don't give up on you, even when you behave badly.

> The staff show you love. Even how rude I was, how intimidating I can be, the staff still embrace you with certain type of care. I started to feel ashamed of myself. I didn't want to be so horrible to the staff because they weren't horrible back. I started looking at myself. I started doing things I'd never done before, go to college, go to the doctor. I started to see my health get better.

Offenders commented on the difference it made just to have someone who listened to them. Caffey said,

> Staff have been supportive and caring. They won't just drop a person out like that. The communication, they give you time, they make time.

He appreciated the fact that the support was not just for a short while or by appointment. Staff were available when he needed them. His view was entirely supported by Brendan, talking about a housing project.

> Staff have been good listeners. It's a true story. At all times of the night as well. I couldn't sleep when I first came here and I had so much things to talk about. So many things I had to get off my head. I just came and sat in that office for hours. Then I could sleep.

For many of the young men who had recently left prison there was a particular value in the lack of prejudice and judgment shown by the staff members. Both Gary and Robert commented on this.

> Not patronised. They treat you like a human being. I was at rock bottom. Would still be there without the help.

> Support, not feeling alone, access to training and courses and drugs work, being treated like a person help you to move on in life and be settled.

The availability of a quick and caring response was also much appreciated as was the possibility of just dropping in but many offenders seemed also to appreciate being challenged and being pushed into doing things. Kevin said that he welcomed.

> Having a support worker who is on me case. If I miss appointments they get on to me. If not for them I'd be up and running. If I have anything in my head I can take it out and give it to her. The stability is a sigh of relief.

Or Jes, who said,

> They've always been there for me. Like a dog with a bone. They respect my opinions. I give them the respect they give me. I'm more assertive. Need to be to survive.

For young men leaving prison there was an obvious importance in having time to reflect and to feel safe. It was clear that many were aware of the stigma attached to a prison sentence and several had spoken of the difficulty in getting on with their lives and relating to others. 'People judge you after prison,' said Anwar. Many community-based projects offered a place to be and to have time to think and plan without having to worry about where to sleep or where the next meal might come from. This sort of respite was what was needed for many so that they could think about their own attitudes as well as their plans for the future. Martin spoke of a place which offered

> Stability and structure. Not having to run round looking for places to sleep.

Geoff said,

> It's given me self-confidence, self-respect and brought me in touch with my family.

For Sean,

[It has] given me the ability to look at myself and my behaviour. I don't get upset so quick. I can say how I feel rather than take everything personally and get angry.

Pete said that his project had

Helped me gain confidence. Society owes you nothing but you need help to get life started again.

For Craig,

Things are working out good. Things are coming together. When I came to the project I was settled at first and then things went pear shaped, but I had help and now I'm back on track. Without the help I'd be in the dock or shot or whatever. Coming to a new area has given me a new start. I'm smug and happy.

Trust, stability and responsiveness were all identified as factors that needed to be in place before individuals could properly look at themselves and where they were going. 'Being stable,' said Majid. 'It's been ten years since I've had any stability.'

Simon was surprised by the responsiveness he found.

They actually come if you call. You feel that. Feel wanted.

Pete also welcomed the sense of mutual trust and the fact that there was someone who was genuinely concerned about him.

Trust. Good that someone cares.

In this sort of background many offenders were able to reflect on what they had been, gain confidence and begin to think where they should go next. In some cases this was simple:

They have helped me to gain confidence.

For Mick it was

Looking at the consequences of your actions.

Colm said,

At first you think you can manage alone and then things go wrong. They got me straight back. Will step aside when you're OK but still there.

It had often been a case of

Providing support, safety and security; shelter and friendly faces; till you're fine on your own.

For some there were substantial achievements. Neil said,

I have completed a computer course and started another. I was a chaotic drug user and would never have had the motivation and commitment without the help I've received.

Will had been grateful for

…not judging people for what they have done in the past but helping people to move forwards towards a positive future.

Life change for many young offenders involves overcoming addiction to alcohol and drugs, which, in many cases, had had a direct impact on their behaviour. Jonno said,

I'll try to get back with me dad on construction. I was drinking all day and night and got the sack. Might be different. I haven't been drinking. Haven't wanted a drink.

Jamie was very much aware that he needed to overcome his drinking problem which had led him to commit crime.

Just with the drink. It span out of control it did. I was shoplifting from shops for ages, getting money just to get a bottle do you know what I mean? To pay for my drink. I was living in a hostel, it was just crap, so I just got into my alcoholic world. Half the time, I'd drink with my mates then go and do my own thing, they'd stop drinking but I carried on drinking myself.

Chris also realised that he needed to

Keep off the heroin and get a job. Last time I went back on it. It's the first few weeks that are the most difficult.

One young man had been using crack cocaine since he was 13-years-old and knew that it was going to be hard to stay clean.

I am worried about getting into drugs again. But if you stay away from them you're alright. If you hang around the people that do them you're going to be doing them in't ya? So it's best just keep away.

Dave agreed with the sentiment.

It isn't something I'm proud of. It's something I deeply regret because it's why I'm back (in prison). I was driving someone to get drugs so it's why I'm back pure and simple. But I did end up getting back with that person … that person has had a history of drugs for almost ten years. It's something I've tried to help her get off and I've tried myself … at the end of the day, when I got back with her … we agreed that none of us would take drugs any more. I'd been clean for a long time. But it didn't work.

Drugs had played a major part in the lives of Dean and Jon.

Stopped going to school at about 14. Started playing truant and fighting. Got into drugs.

I was a model student at about 13 or 14. I started drinking and smoking stuff and it all went wrong. I don't know what it was all about.

The realisation that it is difficult to change led Josh to say,

> I have been helped very much. Wouldn't have managed without help. If people are going to get into trouble they will be less likely if there is someone to talk to, someone to guide them.

Of course, it can be argued that all the help in the world will not make a difference to someone who is not ready to change and Dave pointed out that

> Help is there if you are ready to stop offending but for some the mind set hasn't reached that point so they fail and end up in trouble or in prison.

And desistance is a long term process, not a straightforward and smooth path. Kelvin had a long-term problem with drugs but had tried to get off them:

> I went away for six months to Australia to get away from crack. I went to some backwater place, beautiful, 300 acres. I lived like a king and I didn't think about crack. As soon as I got back in the place ... I said to the black cab driver take that right [to a dealer]. What I learned through my experiences is its not where they send you, it's not about where you are it's where you're at. Where you're at in your mind. I never believed I could do this, stay off drugs, on my doorstep. I went to Bournemouth I couldn't do it, lasted six months. I went to Australia lasted six months. Now I've stayed clean.

His comments highlight the roller-coaster element in change of any sort. Beating an addiction for six months only to start again is a familiar enough scenario for any addict. Desistance from crime is arguably the same. There may be a break in offending only for someone to give in to temptation a year down the line. Desistance may not be in absolute terms. Offending may be less serious, happen less often but what is clear is that there has to be some intention to stop, some acceptance of what is socially acceptable behaviour and what is not. It could be argued that if it is only fear of consequences that makes someone stop offending they are still quite capable of committing more crime. They simply need to be sure that the crime cannot be detected.

Real desistance is more likely to stem from being older and developing a greater sense of the impact of actions on others. Maruna (2000) points out that none of the general theories provide much help in deciding what to do to encourage desistance. Rehabilitation theory has traditionally been seen as something that is quite distinct for desistance but this has meant, Maruna argues, that 'by concentrating almost exclusively on the question of "what works" offender rehabilitation research has largely ignored questions about how rehabilitation works, why it works with some and why it fails with others' (Maruna 2000). His argument is that there is a need for a marriage of the research in order to design interventions that enhance or complement spontaneous efforts to desist. The failure to do this has resulted in the often quoted anecdote concerning the young prisoner who has acquired basic literacy skills through repeated prison sentences but shown no intention of changing his lifestyle, so that the outcome is a burglar who can read.

The provision of practical help and the opportunity to gain practical skills need to be supported by attempts to deal with the attitudes and motivation of the young offender. Equally important is that the young offender who wants to desist should not be prevented from doing so because the interventions and support are not available to him or her and because a failure to address practical difficulties imposes real barriers to the desired desistance. There has to be a link between desistance and rehabilitation so that the one is reinforced by the other. Motivation is not enough when the reality is unreasonably hard.

Economic pressures make it more difficult for young offenders to find work and to find affordable places to live. The same pressures threaten the programmes, interventions and support networks that may make the difference between persevering and giving up. Many of the services available are provided through voluntary organizations, constantly struggling to make ends meet on insecure and short-term funding. Efficiency savings and cuts make it less likely that prisons will be able to provide the rehabilitation and resettlement planning that should run alongside desistance. As if to demonstrate how long this has been an issue Charles Dickens, once again, understood it all. In the novel *Oliver Twist*, Bill Sikes, the burglar, laments the loss of a boy small enough to get through a small window. 'I want a boy, and it mustn't be a big un. Lord!' said Mr Sikes, reflectively.

If I'd only got that boy of Ned, the chimbley-sweeper's! He kept him small on purpose, and let him out by the job. But the father gets lagged; and then the Juvenile Delinquent Society comes, and takes the boy from a trade where he was earning money, teaches him to read and write, and in time makes a 'prentice of him. 'And so they go on', said Mr Sikes, his wrath rising with the recollection of his wrongs, 'so they go on; and, if they'd got money enough (which it's a Providence they haven't,) we shouldn't have half-a dozen boys left in the whole trade, in a year or two'.

The book was serialised in 1837-9 and it marked the start of Dickens' indictment of the cruelty that children suffer at the hands of society. It is a brutal fact that so many years later children and young people are denied the opportunity to learn skills and to find employment and training, while the institutions and organizations that might help them are without sufficient funding to do it adequately.

CHAPTER FOUR

FAMILY, WHAT FAMILY?

> They fuck you up your Mum and Dad
> They may not mean to but they do
> They fill you with the faults they had
> And add some extra just for you.
>
> Philip Larkin

Health and safety at work experts are usually insistent that not only accidents in the workplace but also near misses should be recorded. The benefit is that it is possible to learn from the mistake that nearly resulted in accident and to make other workers aware that there is a risk in an action or activity.

Life, for most people, is full of near misses. Careful and caring but momentarily inattentive parents find themselves in A and E because their child has fallen downstairs, been scalded, tripped over the doorstep or fallen out of a tree. Most drivers, normally careful and sensible will own up to the occasion when they pulled out in front of an oncoming car because they didn't see it coming. In most cases the child has bruises or blisters and the inattentive driver gets gestures from the other driver but no harm is done. Parents and drivers become more aware and vigilant as a result, at least for a time and no long-term harm is done. Every now and then the near miss is an accident with serious consequences which may have an impact on the individual for the rest of their lives.

Sometimes it seems to be no more than good luck or bad luck that determines whether the accident happens and whether the result is minor or very serious indeed. Sometimes the difference is that there is some intervention that prevents a serious consequence. In Jerome's case the comments of a police woman and her decision not to push him into the criminal justice system meant that Jerome learned an early lesson without serious consequences to himself or anyone else.

I started to get into trouble when I was about 15. Not serious but stupid stuff. Trouble at school. Bit of shoplifting. Then I got picked up by this woman police officer. She just told me off. Told me not to do stuff again. Said there was no need. I could do good stuff instead. I never really got involved with much after that and I sorted the school bit and got my GCSEs.

Jason's experience was rather different. For him the fact that he had, unintentionally, caused someone a serious injury meant that he was projected through the criminal justice system.

There was a fight outside the pub. There were loads of people there. I didn't even want to get into it. I was chatting up this girl, but then I just did get into it and I hit this bloke. I broke his jaw. So the police came and loads of people just went away but someone said I hit this bloke and bust his jaw and so the police picked me up and here I am inside.

It is inevitable that a developing child will put themselves at risk. Children explore, they climb, and they investigate how machinery works. Forbidden areas are a temptation. Why else do medicines have child proof locks? If things go wrong most children have a caring parent who will administer first aid or take them to the hospital or just give them a cuddle to make things better. That is not available to children who have parents who are not caring or are not attentive for whatever reason. When the family life the child experiences is not loving and supportive there is a real sense that matters will go from bad to worse as early disadvantages are compounded over and over again.

A case study taken from a report on Nacro's On Side project demonstrates this cumulative disadvantage and just how much is needed to try to mitigate the damage that has been caused. The study describes a young man who was serving a 15 month sentence for burglary. He said that he had started offending when he was 12 or 13, starting with shoplifting and moving on to car thefts and a conviction for arson. He believed he had about 27 convictions and had committed over 60 offences. He had been in custody before. He was one of five children brought up in the South West. His parents had separated when he was a toddler. When he was eleven his mother and her boyfriend went on holiday, leaving the children to look after themselves. The neighbours alerted the authorities and he and his younger brother were placed in care. He said that this was when he started to offend.

> Childhood really, going into care, not going to school properly. Well. I can't say I haven't had a good bring up cos I did, but not in the way I would have liked it, a bit better, if you know what I mean. With my mum and dad splitting up all the time, not seeing my dad since well, 12 or 13 months ago for the first time. Not having a dad around.

He had been in and out of care and had attended school irregularly. He said that he never attended a 'proper school' but was sent to a school considered better able to handle his frequent losses of temper and difficulty managing his anger. He said he was tutored at home from the age of 12 but had no formal qualifications. He could read and write and had no desire to continue with education, explaining,

> I can't be bothered to sit down and do it, now I'm getting older I want to get on with life and that.

He had been introduced to cannabis, aged 12, by his older brother and by the age of 17 was using cocaine, pills and heroin. He had also sold cocaine in the past. Alcohol had been a problem, especially after he decided to reduce his drug use. Asked if he drank much, he said,

> I would say no but, I'd like to say no but I don't know. During resettlement last week telling them how much I drink and then working it out on paper with units and that I was like, 'Whoa!'. Do you know what I mean? That's made me think a bit more, just like, what's the point of drinking that much? Just drink to go out and get drunk? Now I've realised it's go out and have a good time and not get drunk…Drink makes you do crime, well, doesn't make you do it, but gives you more the edge. No I can't do that any more.

His project officer had made three referrals to the Counselling, Assessment, Referral, Advice and Throughcare team (CARATs) in the prison but he had not been seen by them. The project worker was, therefore, undertaking a drug work package with him in one to one sessions.

This young man's brother had been murdered and this had added to the stress and worry he experienced. He felt increasingly responsible for his mother who was said to have health problems, mental health problems and substance misuse issues. He had become depressed after his brother's death but it had made him realise how his actions had affected his mother and how

> My mother's the only thing I've got left. We've got to look after each other.

He had not really grieved for his brother and there was some concern that he would seek to get revenge on those who he thought were responsible for his brother's death. His project worker was going to attend some of the trial with him, after his release, to provide moral support and to try to ensure that he did not allow his anger to get the better of him.

He was at great risk of leaving prison homeless, as he could not return to live with his mother and had split up with the girlfriend with whom he had been living before he was sentenced.

An application was made to a housing project and temporary release on licence was arranged for the interview. The application was, however, deferred because they did not feel he showed sufficient commitment. He explained,

> They didn't say they'd refused me, they said they'd deferred it cos they don't think I've got enough a sensible head, not in them words, but I don't think I've got enough of a sensible head to find work or training, cos I told them when I get out I ain't going straight to work cos I need time, I've been here eight months. I need time to settle down and see my family, like my mum, my friends and that. I need a week out or something and then go back to work. They said 'Ah no, we don't think you're going to do that, you're going to come out and commit crime again'.

He thought he was going to be living with a friend of his mother's but instead he went to a bed and breakfast near his mother's home. He was pleased with it.

The project worker kept in touch after release and still helped with accommodation. He moved back in with his girlfriend and was looking for a flat for both of them. His project officer supplied a list of private landlords in the area. He also wanted employment. He had previously worked as a plasterer and wanted that work again. The project officer helped him write to his previous employer and he was taken on again. He also got a small grant to help with tools, though these were later stolen from the boot of his car. He was grateful for the help he had received from his project officer and he wanted to keep in touch with after release. He appreciated the advice he had been given:

> If you ain't got money, just accept that you ain't got money, don't go out and commit crime and disappoint someone else…along them sort of lines. Its made me think. All the other ones…just sit there 'yeah you thieve, it's your fault you got banged up. I'll be there to breach you' and nothing else. She's not like that. She speaks to you and helps you come to terms with what you've done wrong. Teaches you not to do it no more. Well, nobody can teach you, you've got to help yourself, but she can give you advice to do that. She's alright. I get on well with her.

He wanted to keep in touch on release and said he would like her to know how he was doing. 'I can show her I can do it'. He thought that if he had had the kind of support he was now getting earlier in his life it might have

> …kept me in school, kept me out of trouble.

He was optimistic about the future and thought that he was unlikely to re-offend though he was realistic about how hard this might be. Asked to say on a scale of one to ten how likely he was to offend he said,

> I can't say one cos that would be lying to myself but I'll say two because in the near future I could be in really serious money troubles with some drug dealer or something, not that I want to but I can't predict the future can I? I don't want to commit crime but I can't predict the future. I've just got to keep going every day as it comes, just work, work, work!

This case study is taken from the evaluation report on the project and at that time he was living in the community and was working as a labourer.

In adolescence risk-taking and experimentation is normal. It seems that especially for boys there is a need to try things out, to take chances and to deliberately defy authority. When that defiance goes too far it is often the response from the adolescent and from parents that makes the difference to the outcome. Misbehaviour in school provides a clear example. The child whose parents come to the school to discuss any problem with the teacher, who are supportive and interested and who will contribute to resolving any problems is far more likely to stay in the school and to be dealt with within the school framework than the child whose parents refuse to co-operate or who become angry or violent towards teaching staff. The actual behaviour may have been the same but the consequences very different.

In 1998 Nacro produced a report called 'Wasted Lives'. Introducing the report the then Chief Executive, Helen Edwards, said,

> Wasted Lives is about boys who commit crimes and end up in prison. The report describes their backgrounds and characteristics and adds up how much their offending costs society. It finds that a great deal of their offending arises from severe family, health and education problems, with high levels of drug use and violence an accepted part of their lives.

> While this in no way excuses crime, it shows the problems that we must tackle if we are serious about reducing it. The report shows that many opportunities to attack these problems early have been missed leaving the criminal justice system to pick up the pieces as best it can. Support and training for their parents and measures to improve attendance at school could have made a deal of difference to these boys' lives. And while this would have cost something, the interventions would have repaid dividends with fewer crimes, fewer victims and less work for criminal justice agencies later on.

Of course there can be no guarantee that early interventions would have eradicated problems for these young men nor that some at least would not have continued to commit crime but the brief profiles of the young men contained in the report do strongly suggest that if there had been some help early in their lives some mistakes could have been avoided and, even if made the consequences might have been less severe.

In the first profile a 15-year-old Irish 'traveller' was sentenced to a term of ten months imprisonment for an offence of burglary. He had many previous convictions for offences including burglary, assault and escape from custody. He thought he got into trouble because there 'was no one out there to tell me what to do'. He thinks he would take notice of his mother but she is in Ireland. His father had died seven years before. He had an older brother and cousins in England but they were all in prison. He had travelled around England and Ireland all his life and had left school at the age of 12.

Another profile described a young man, aged 15, who was serving a sentence of 15 months for stealing money from a betting shop. He had a number of previous convictions for robbery and assault. He said that he had started to offend when he was 12 by taking money from a petrol station cashier. He was expelled from school for fighting at the age of 14. He was taken into the care of the local authority at the age of nine following physical and sexual abuse by his father. Any money he got from offending he spent on drugs and clothes.

A third example is that of a 17-year-old serving a two year sentence for a savage assault, although it was his first conviction. Many of his friends had been in trouble and some are in prison. His family life centred around an older sister and his mother and was punctuated by visits from his father who was abusive and violent towards him and his mother. He experienced further violence when his mother acquired a new and abusive boyfriend. He was placed on the at-risk register when he was 14. A year later he was taken into care. He was expelled from school for non-attendance.

These examples are taken from a report that is over ten years old but the sad fact is that offenders interviewed much more recently are describing circumstances which are very similar. These circumstances may not excuse crime but they do make it easier to understand how young men become vulnerable to becoming involved in crime.

Mikey explained that his parents had split up just over a year before but

> …it was bad before that. He used to knock her about but she wanted to stay until all of us kids had grown up. I don't know where I can go when I get out. No one

wants to talk to me about it. I got in trouble at school. I had a knife and used it
on this kid. I didn't hurt him bad but I got done for it and now I'm in here.

Violence in the home was a factor for Jimmy who had lived with his father
after his parents separated.

Me dad was in and out of prison. He used to knock me about when he was home.
I was bad in school. I was a bully. Got expelled from a few schools. Started crime
when I was about ten. Used to go out with me brothers.

Jamil came to England when he was ten.

I came to live with my aunt. My mother died. She didn't want me, sent me
into care. They don't care about you there either. I don't see my family. I've got
brothers and my father. I don't see him.

Peter's mother died when he was very young. He lives with his father and
his older brother. Both of them are violent and abusive men. Peter's own
violence has resulted in school exclusion and a number of convictions for
assault. He has a great deal of trouble controlling his temper and is quite
unpredictable when he does lose it. He tried to settle down briefly.

I had a girlfriend and we had a baby. She went off with someone else when I did
my last sentence. I still want to see the baby. Don't know if she'll let me.

Carl explained that he had spent time in boarding schools.

Bad schools for bad boys. I used to be with my mum but then I went to my aunt.
I did know my father but I never lived with him. My mum had another bloke
but he used to beat her. I hated him and he hated me. Couldn't stay with them.'

When his mother ran off with another man, Craig was very angry with her.

I never saw her again. I was with me dad but he got another woman and after
that I went into care. I've been in trouble since I was about 12.

Dave is 17 and serving a 24 month sentence. It is his second time in custody and he has a number of convictions dating back to his early teens.

> I never saw my real father. I had a step father but he used to beat me. My mother she never did anything to stop him. Nothing to help me. I don't want to see her any more.

There was a history of violence in Darren's family too.

> My parents split up. There was a lot of violence before. I went with me dad but it didn't work out. Did go to me mum but I got in with a crowd. Bad crowd. Things just went wrong from there.

One young man described the way in which he started offending when he was living rough.

> I just didn't have any money. Needed food. I never got on with my parents or my brother. He's inside now. I got into trouble at school as well. Got expelled after the first time I was inside.

Jack is serving six months. His home life was unhappy. His mother had never accepted him and she emotionally and physically abused him.

> I used to spend time with friends . I need friends so I can stay with them. If I try to go home she'll just throw me out again.

Ian chose to stay with his father when his parents split up.

> We didn't really get on but I wanted to stay with my friends. My mum moved away. Me brothers and sister went with her. I got into loads of trouble at school. Just got fed up with it. Couldn't be arsed. Got expelled anyway.

What emerges from these comments, whether they were made over ten years ago or whether they come from more recent interviews, is that a disruptive and unhappy home life has a massive long-term impact on the children of the family. Many of the young men speak of violence and abuse and, in many cases, their own violence and aggression is merely a mirror image of behaviour that they have seen in the home.

Helen Edwards was right to say that this does not excuse involvement in crime but to start life from a position of such disadvantage must make it less easy to avoid involvement, especially when that early disadvantage is so often compounded over and over again.

Aggression and unhappiness has also led to problems in their relationships with others so that exclusion from school has often been as a consequence of violence to others; both to teachers and other pupils.

Home, in many cases, was also home to others already involved in the criminal justice system. Many speak of fathers, mothers and older brothers who are currently serving prison sentences. One young man said,

> I've been reading loads since I've been inside. My mum and my older brothers have all been inside and they all said 'read'. It makes the time go.

Not the sort of advice that you might expect a mother to be giving her son. At the age of ten and eleven Matt and his brother were sent out by their father to steal and were beaten if they did not come back with money. Not a great role model for a child.

And if you have run away from home because you are abused, been thrown out because you can't get on with your step-father or your mother hates you, where do you go? Several of the young men spoke of being in care but they also spoke of a lack of care by social workers and breakdowns in fostering arrangements. Often they accepted that their own behaviour had been such that foster parents could not cope with them. Tom had been in several foster homes.

> I stayed with some people who weren't bad to me but I was so angry about everything that I just wanted to smash things up all the time. The foster people said they couldn't cope with me and so I got moved but it was never right. I always got moved again.

Problems at home had all too often spilled over into school. Sometimes this was because the violent behaviour at home was acted out in school but sometimes just because it was hard to concentrate on what the teacher was saying when there were so many worries and concerns about life at home.

'I got into a lot of trouble at school,' said Jamie.

> I see now I was a pain in the arse but then I was just so angry about all the stuff that was happening at home. I know I was bad but why didn't the teachers ever ask me if there was something wrong. Maybe I wouldn't have told them. I don't know. But they could have asked instead of just seeing how I was and thinking I was a prat and not worth bothering with.

Out of school, out of home. A far cry from Rutherford's concern that we should 'hold on to a young person' until they grow out of crime. Early disadvantage breeds more and more disadvantage until the opportunity to behave differently, to learn to behave differently, begins to be worn away.

Without a family to provide some sort of code, some morality as well as some basic emotional and practical care for the child the burden falls increasingly on the school where the child goes next. But the child who goes to the school is unprepared for its discipline and its rules. For the child who comes from a family where there has been little dialogue and limited opportunity to develop language skills it is likely that much of what a teacher says will be incomprehensible. Jon said,

> They said I was rude in school. I didn't think I was but there was so much yes sir, no sir, please sir, thank you sir I got pissed off with it. The teacher used to give you this lecture if you did anything wrong. I couldn't understand half what she said. She just went on and on. I didn't listen to half of it.

The Institute for Public Policy Research (IPPR) report 'Make Me a Criminal' published in 2008 includes truanting or being expelled from school as risk factors in offending and conversely suggests that enjoying the school experience and getting a lot from it is a protective factor. School potentially offers structure, something to do, a place to be and the opportunity to learn new skills and to achieve. When school breaks down the child is denied all of those things as well as the loss of opportunity to gain the qualifications that could lead to further education or to employment.

The Social Exclusion Unit, reporting in 2002, highlighted the extent to which offenders were a disadvantaged group before they ever came into contact with the criminal justice system. The report demonstrates the extent to which prisoners are more likely than the general population to have had disrupted experiences of education and to have left school without qualifications and with low basic skills. It is, therefore, not a surprise to find that few prisoners have ever experienced regular or high quality employment. The report cites a figure of 67% of prisoners being unemployed against 5% of the general population.

Employment is of great importance in reducing the risk of offending or re-offending. A stable job reduces the chances of re-offending by one third to one half, demonstrating just how important it is that offenders have an opportunity to find and keep employment. Low basic skills and lack of qualifications will have made it more difficult to find work prior to any convictions but having a criminal record, especially when the record includes a prison sentence, make finding work nigh on impossible for many offenders. The knowledge that disclosure of a criminal record will lead to rejection by potential employers makes many young offenders unwilling to try to find work. Mark said that he had repeatedly tried to find work

> …but I had nothing. Never had a job so they said no experience. Got no qualifications. Then once you've got a criminal record you can forget it anyway.

The prospect of approaching an employer expecting the answer no is a daunting prospect. Some will try to get round the problem by not disclosing offences. This is a high risk strategy because it involves, effectively, lying to the employer. Many offenders say that although they were able to find work they lost it as soon as the employer found out about the convictions, either through a record check or because someone informed on them. This is what had happened to David, even though he had been working well at a local factory for some time.

I didn't tell them I had a record. Everywhere else I went I had told them and they didn't want to know me. So this time I didn't say anything and I got the job. I was doing Ok and then some busybody says to the boss that I had a record. That was the end of the job.

There is no doubt that criminal record checks are necessary. No employer will want to recruit someone whose criminal record is relevant to the type of work on offer and who may present a risk to other workers or to anyone else. However, the process often operates unfairly so that offenders are rejected because of an offence which is old and or irrelevant or because the offence appears, on paper, to have been more serious than it really was. Even when convictions are spent some employers will still insist on disclosure, even where there is no legal right for them to have that information. The result is that offenders are rejected at interview or are dismissed as soon as their record comes to light. It seems a particular irony that the impact of disclosure hits at the very people who are trying to find work, who are trying not to be involved in crime. A 'hardened criminal' is unlikely to be looking for legitimate full time employment.

Lack of employment is a problem not only because it means financial hardship but also because employment provides structure and status. For many young men finding work is crucial to their identity as a man and as an adult. Without a realistic prospect of employment there is less incentive to move away from old friends and offending habits. One young man said that one of the benefits he found from working was that

...I can say to people I can't come out drinking every night of the week. I have to get up for work in the morning.

He said that drinking had been very much tied up with his offending and the fact of a job was giving him a chance to give up on both.

Without sufficient income, housing becomes even more of a problem. Young people in general are finding it harder to afford their own homes and are staying longer in their parents' homes. This is often not an option for young offenders where the parental home may be a part of their problem. The Social Exclusion Unit report cites research suggesting that stable accommodation can reduce re-offending by 20%. Ian commented that having somewhere decent to live meant that he had something to lose.

> Once you've got a place you don't want to screw up and lose it.

Many young offenders are forced to sleep rough or to sleep on the floor with various friends. This does not make for a stable or settled existence and it increases the problem in accessing other services. An address is necessary in order to register with a GP for example. In fact many would argue that having a place to live is the essential need for any young offender and that without it nothing else will happen.

There are occasions when a young offender can return to live with their parents or other family members. This is not always easy. There are practical difficulties because the fact of an offender in a property can invalidate insurance if it is not declared and will almost certainly increase the cost of household insurance. Nor is it always easy to live with a young offender. Parents sometimes speak of being worried that their son's friends or former friends will be visiting the house. One desperate mother spoke of feeling guilty that she was pleased when her son received a custodial sentence because she had been so worried about his thefts from her handbag and about his anger if she tried to place any restrictions on his behaviour.

The research literature points consistently to a chain of events which build disadvantage on disadvantage. Young men from disadvantaged backgrounds start out with an increased risk of becoming involved in crime and, once involved, further disadvantages make it ever harder to desist and to live differently. This accumulation of disadvantages creates huge barriers to desistance so that even when a young offender genuinely wants to stop offending it is increasingly difficult for him or her to do so.

In a second example, taken from the On Side report a young man was serving a 21 month sentence for burglary. He had nine previous convictions for offences such as burglary, drug-related offences, violence against the person and theft but he thought he had probably committed hundreds of offences in his lifetime.

He said that he had become involved in crime through drugs and peer pressure and that his offending had started when he was 15.

I got into the wrong crowd when I was about 13. One minute I was outside the group then I was like in the middle of the group. I got really bad into the group and started burgling houses and doing stuff what I shouldn't have been doing.

He had started using drugs aged 12, using cannabis at first and then moving on to develop a £500 per week crack cocaine habit by the age of 15. His drug use and his involvement in crime led to a breakdown in the relationship between his mother and step-father and he had not lived at home with his mother for the last four years. He said that this was his choice because he felt guilty about the constant police attention his behaviour brought on the family. He then lived with friends just sleeping on their floors.

He had not been in touch with his biological father for some 15 years but he had been in touch again during the sentence. He was pleased to have the contact with his father and was placing increasing reliance on him but he was stressed by the fact that his mother did not know about the contact Despite a disrupted childhood he had never been in care or on the child protection register.

He had stopped going to school when he was 13 and began smoking cannabis. He said that no-one ever tried to get him back into the classroom because his mother and the teachers thought he was attending.

During his sentence he was placed on medication by prison health staff because he was 'hearing voices' and he had been considered a risk of suicide/self-harming by some of the staff. He was housed on the Coping Skills Unit within the prison and seemed to enjoy the relationships between prison staff and inmates there.

The officers on my wing are very supportive and that, cos there's only four staff to 31 inmates so they help you through each day. If you've got a problem you just go and tell them and they sort it out for you and everything's alright!

Assessment by the project team showed that he needed help and support around drug use, employment, peer group pressures, accommodation and persistent offending. He was to be accommodated in a supported project on his release. This seemed a sensible option, though he was encouraged to work on his relationship with his mother, with his project officer facilitating phone calls between them.

The project officer also explored training and employment opportunities, including a fork lift truck driving course.

After his release he stayed in touch with his project officer and was doing well at his supported project but he was finding it hard to break the drug habit.

> I thought, 'Why am I doing this? Shall I just scarper off and do what I want to do? Just jump out of the car and just go?' That's what I was thinking all the way here, 'Shall I just go and get some crack?' All the way back…because I had crack on the brain, it was the first day out. Went into jail cracked out of my head and wanted to get out of jail cracked out of my head as well, but I'm glad I did come here because I haven't touched it since. Which is good for me really, I've been on crack since I was 13.

He was very positive about the help he had received from his project officer:

> Helping me find this place, helping me think straight when I was down and out and thought I was never going to get out of jail, he'd help me think, 'Yeah, you'll be out sooner or later, you've only got three months left and you can do that on your head, you've done eight months'. I don't know, just talking and talking to me and helping me get through it. In jail you can have a good month and you can have a bad month, it all depends what happens. He was there to reassure me.

He had never experienced such support before saying that his project officer

> …is like a mentor, sort of thing, that's what I think cos he's the only person who has helped me the whole time.

He had never had support during previous prison sentences or when he was younger and first involved in crime. He thought he would have benefited from some support sooner, though he recognised that when he was younger he was

…just right off my head…didn't give a care in the world about no one.

Three months after his release he had not committed any offences. Previously the longest period had been six weeks and he was proud that he had stayed out of trouble and off crack. However, he said, 'it gets harder every day'. He knew that there was a risk that he would return to drugs and to crime but said,

If I ever offend again, I'll probably feel ashamed about it this time. All the other times, when I come into prison this time I didn't really care about no-one. I just thought when I get out I'll do the same thing over and over again. But the project officer helped me through that, got me off the pattern of getting out, committing crime and coming back in again. Hopefully I'll be able to sort myself out.

He had had no contact from his mother since his release from prison and his birth father had only been in touch sporadically. He was troubled by this and felt let down by his parents. This hindered his progress and after five months he was recalled under his release licence, for drug dealing, and was returned to custody. His case demonstrates just how hard it is to give up on addiction and to go straight. Support from the project had helped him but it was not quite enough to counteract the difficulty and the lack of support that he had from his parents.

Clearly there is a need to remove the barriers if we want to reduce the risks of future offending. Ideally there should be early intervention so that this chain of disadvantage is broken early in life. Investment in support for parents and for young people themselves and in resources for schools is needed so that there is more scope to engage and motivate the cynical and the disaffected. This is an argument that has been promoted by many and for many years. It is an argument that is not always heeded and we continue to see young men at high risk of becoming involved in crime being projected all too rapidly into and through the criminal justice system.

Much that needs to be done to prevent crime is never going to be provided through the criminal justice system. Education, social care, housing and employment all of which are hugely significant in reducing crime are nothing to do with a criminal justice system. For some young men the extent of their offending or the seriousness of it will inevitably bring them before the criminal courts and the acquisition of a record that will make life even harder. Offenders themselves frequently acknowledge that there was little choice about this. Their behaviour could not go unpunished and ignored. So what needs to be in place to ensure that the way in which young men are treated once they are involved in the criminal justice system does not simply make matters worse?

CHAPTER FIVE

NOTHING TO DO, NOTHING TO LOSE, MUCH TO GAIN

> ... Though justice be thy plea, consider this,
> That in the course of justice none of us
> Should see salvation ...
>
> Shakespeare, *The Merchant of Venice.*

During the latter part of 2010 we heard a great deal about 'lifestyle choice'. The implication of this is that people can choose to be poor, to be unemployed and to offend. Young offenders appear not to disagree with the concept entirely. Many of them comment that, ultimately, the decision to offend and, more significantly, to stop offending is a personal decision, a matter of choice.

The reality is that for the most part we are not talking about real choice or fair choice. It is easier to choose to be employed if you have the skills and qualifications to find the job. It is easier to choose not to offend when you have parents who support you and provide you with the basic necessities of life as well as with love and care. Many young offenders will have started life in a position of disadvantage and it is hard to believe that there could ever be any sense of choice for the child who lives with abusive or neglectful parents.

What might be a more acceptable concept of choice would be one where that includes the mitigation of disadvantage and which offers real opportunity for a young person to choose to do something different. Many young people who misbehave during adolescence and may even be involved in some crime will be given an opportunity to change before they become involved in the criminal justice system to any significant degree. They will have parents who step in to help or there will be another adult in their lives who offers them some support and guidance or just acts as a sensible role model. In an ideal world we should be looking to provide such opportunities at an early age, not just because children might become offenders but also because every child has a right to a decent start in life and the opportunity to achieve their own goals and ambitions. It is not, of course, an ideal world and there are always going to be young people who do move through the system and into the realm of criminal justice.

While it is true that involvement in the criminal justice system can create further disadvantage and research suggests that early involvement is very likely to make matters worse, it would be foolish to deny that there is potential for services accessed through the criminal justice system to help and support young people. Many of the services provided for young offenders are only available because of a referral by a probation officer, implying an involvement in crime before the service is available. There are penalties that include elements that will contribute to helping the individual. Requirements to attend anger management courses, referrals to rehabilitation (often just 're-hab') or to drug advice services might be included in this. There are initiatives that are designed to create a choice between offending and not offending.

One of the key factors in these initiatives appears to be the 'joining up' of services; a model where a variety of agencies work together, collaborating completely to provide both co-ordination of activities and a wide range of expertise. The model makes it possible to access the various services that an individual needs in order to reduce the risk of their re-offending. There will also be a police awareness of the individual and evocation of sanctions if there is a further crime. A crude description would be that there is provision to meet the many needs of the individual offender and so offer a genuine opportunity to go straight, if that option is not going to be taken up there is an 'or else' that kicks in, in the form of arrest and further charges.

A senior officer from Greater Manchester once described an initiative introduced to deal with the serious problems of gang crime. The police targeted gang leaders, often those for whom criminal behaviour was firmly entrenched, doing, he said 'what the police do best'. They arrested those leaders so that they were removed, at least for a while, from the local area. This made it possible for other organizations to work with young people who wanted to get out of the gang culture but were too afraid of reprisals to take that step. It also benefited young people who were on the periphery and likely to be sucked in. Some of the organizations and individuals providing the help were themselves former gang members who had the knowledge and credibility to influence younger people. Desmond had been involved in a gang when he was younger but was now working on a project designed to help young people to leave the gang culture. He said,

> I don't think that people realise that if you are in an area where gangs are operating it can be very hard to stay out of it and harder still to leave it once you are in. A lot of kids won't leave because they are afraid. If gang leaders are picked up it gives us a real opportunity to get in and talk to some of the younger ones. They will take it from me because I've been there myself. No disrespect to some of the people who work for the agencies round here but they haven't been there and the kids know that. It's all about your credibility. There are other organizations that can help them with finding a place to live and all that but I think they need someone who really knows what it's like to get them off the gang crime thing in the first place.

Rob had also been an offender when he was younger. He had been involved in a project, which had offered him the opportunity to take up white water rafting. He explained how he had moved on from there.

> It was a bit of a coincidence really that I got the chance to do this residential activity course. I hadn't ever done anything like it but we went out on the river and it was just amazing. It gave me such a buzz. I just got more involved and I eventually got qualified as an instructor. There are two things that are important when I do the activities with the kids. First it is exciting for them. They never come to me saying they are bored. Scared sometimes but not bored! The second thing is that I was into crime when I was a kid. I know where they are coming from and they can see me and know that it is possible to do something different.

The Street Weapons Commission report published in 2008 described an initiative in Hackney, where a Curb Offender Management Unit (COMU) has been established. The unit aims to tackle violence among young people by pro-actively targeting known offenders. It works in partnership with the local council, youth support teams, the Mobile Gang Intervention Team (MIT), Safer Schools Partnerships, the Learning Trust and others. At any one time there will be 30 named individuals broken down into three tiers.

- High: Regular offenders who are unwilling to engage in intervention or diversion. They are subject to all available enforcement tactics including stop and search by the police, anti-social behaviour orders (ASBOs), revocation of tenancies and arrest.

- Medium: those who are coming to the attention of the police but can actively be engaged; the aim is to prevent and deter them and move them down a tier using the MIT.

- Early intervention: those at risk of gang involvement or becoming victims of violence who come to their attention through bullying, being bullied or as victims. Helped using youth support teams.

Those in the highest tier are seen by police officers on a regular basis and surveillance is intensive. COMU and MIT work together to reinforce the message that violent and gang-related behaviour will not be tolerated and where enforcement of statutory court orders is needed this will be taken. When behaviour improves, they are returned to medium tier risk and rewards such as access to activities is given.

After the first six months there was an 18% reduction in violence. A public attitude survey in 2007-2008 showed that 73% of Hackney residents felt safe when walking alone in the area after dark. This figure rose to 96% for walking alone during the day.

Research which indicated that a small number of offenders are responsible for a disproportionate amount of all crime led to the introduction of the Prolific and Other Priority Offender (PPO) programme. An evaluation of the programme conducted by Paul Dawson (Home Office 2007) pointed to good practice in dealing with this challenging group of offenders. One of the findings was that there was great value in involving all relevant agencies in identifying PPOs so as to ensure that the programme was targeting the right group of offenders. The report also suggested that co-locating relevant agencies was helpful because it made it much easier for various agencies to work together in a co-ordinated way. The report found that there were clear benefits in partnership working, not least because it appeared that PPOs have specific needs in terms of accommodation, drugs misuse and education, training and employability issues, over and above the needs of other offenders, and that only a multi-agency approach could fulfil the multiple needs. The offenders interviewed for the research were largely positive about the scheme. There were concerns about the enhanced tracking of offenders that formed part of the programme but one young man cited in the report said,

> There was no support in the past—you had to go in once a week to see a probation officer for two minutes—it was like clocking in once a week. All that did was keep you out of prison for a certain amount of time until you get nicked again. Now you get all the help you need.

Another quoted said,

> They said I'd finished and if I need any help just ring them…come back if I need anything – they've already said that…even my drugs worker said…'Any time you need help just ring me'.

A third young man quoted in the impact assessment conducted by Dawson and Cuppleditch (Home Office 2007) said,

> My offending has decreased and in my case, sometimes when I was close to offending I would actually picture the two police officers, they would be in my mind, to think I have to see them this week…it deters you from committing offences just to know that you are going to be seeing police officers.

A police representative provided a case study.

> We picked up one lad who was 17…but he was being released from HMP, he was homeless, he had no clothing, apart from what he stood up in, he had no means of support, no money, no food…The team were no longer working with him because he'd finished his sentence, and it was two weeks prior to his 18th birthday so basically they were opening the prison gates, and just letting this lad out. Totally unsupported. Because he was a PPO we managed to pull together all the agencies and when he actually left prison, he was collected by a youth offending worker who took him to pre-arranged appointments with

> Connexions, with the Benefits Agency. They were all appointments that we'd set up, we secured him accommodation, in supported tenancy, so he had his own little flat, and he had the support of workers within the scheme, we got him a food parcel, just to sort of help him out and we've worked with him intensively….he must have been back in the community about six months now and he's still crime free…and I know last week he had a job interview.

The example helps to demonstrate the beneficial impact of collaborative working, so that there is expertise available to address all the needs of the PPO. It also provides a stark example of the number of needs that must be addressed and serves to demonstrate the extent to which an expectation that a young offender can leave custody and cope adequately without help and support is both unrealistic and cruel. One police officer said,

> The important point is that there has to be a safety net for these kids. And a really tight mesh on it too. It only works if everyone works together and so you can meet real needs. You can't have bad communication, or people being precious about sharing information or not wanting to refer someone to another service. Everyone has to work together. Everyone doing the bits that they do best.'

When the concept of offender management was introduced it seemed to be a genuine way to improve the way in which both offender and crime itself was managed. The principle behind this initiative was that there would be an offender manager, responsible for assessing individual risk and need and commissioning a package of services from a variety of providers in order to meet the needs of the individual. It catered for the reality that most offenders have more than one need and there is little point in dealing with one risk factor if several others remain. It also recognised that no one person or one agency has all the answers or all the skills. Some organizations provide training, others housing, some offer support for drugs and alcohol users and some provide counselling and support services. The reality of the National Offender Management Service (NOMS) fell short of expectations and it has all too rarely provided the sort of service that was needed if it was to effect real change. Bureaucracy, lack of resources, an overworked probation service and some very mixed messages about the notion of competition among organizations have corrupted the concept. The rapidly rising prison population also contributed to the contamination of the concept as prisons struggled to provide the rehabilitative regimes needed in order to comply with offender manager requirements. Prisoners continued to be sent miles away from their homes, there were continuing problems with the transfer of information and, despite the best efforts of many prison and probation staff the concept has not lived up to its promise. The prison estate has been over-used in the United Kingdom to the point of dysfunctionality and the priority must be to find ways to keep people, especially young people, out of such a system. While it is sadly the case that there will always be a proportion of offenders for whom custody is the only option the over use has made it increasingly difficult for prisons to provide the sort of regime that might make a real difference to the possibility of re-offending.

A senior member of HM Prison Service was sceptical about the introduction of the offender management service. He explained why:

> It seemed to assume that the Prison Service was deliberately sending prisoners miles from home, deliberately denying prisoners the opportunity to prepare for release. The truth is that unless you have resources and you have enough staff to deal with the numbers you are just warehousing prisoners. It is almost impossible to offer the sort of regime that is really needed.

A constructive regime can contribute to the rehabilitation of offenders. There is an opportunity to remove some of the barriers to desistance. There is potential to offer programmes and activities that address offending behaviour. There is scope to put things in place in advance of the release date so that a former prisoner does have access to a decent place to live and to employment. If all of this worked consistently across the prison estate we would still have to recognise the potential damage that prison can do even while it tries to rehabilitate. Prisoners frequently leave custody institutionalised, disorientated and vulnerable. Despite good efforts many will not have had access to the programmes that they need and they will not be going out to a home or a job. Some will have lost the job and the home that they had as a result of the sentence and many will have lost contact with their family and friends too. Even at its rehabilitative best, prison is a high price to pay. Reconviction rates tell us that it is not a truly effective way of reducing crime, though it is a very expensive attempt at it.

One famous prisoner stated:

> Prison not only robs you of your identity. Everyone wears a uniform, eats the same food, follows the same schedule. It is by definition a purely authoritarian state that tolerates no independence and individuality.[1]

One young prisoner was bitter about his experiences of prison.

> Since I got here my perspective of prison has changed. I initially though that prisons were a hopeful environment. I've now realised that prisons are full of people who have been persecuted (not prosecuted), victims of peer pressure or people who have just made the wrong decisions. Most of the hostility I have encountered is from the officers here. Not all officers are confrontational but some officers abuse their power and position. I recommend that officers should do communication courses and if staff are available good prisons should get extra incentive schemes.

Ben was soon to be released, having served 15 months and he commented on the failure to act early enough to make a real difference and suggested that any good that prison might offer was too little too late.

> I feel that when you're incarcerated they don't do enough towards youth offending behaviour. When you come to people's attention it's too late.

Other comments suggest a failure to offer constructive help and opportunity.

> Since I have been in here I have been on my best behaviour and have tried to get used to everything and all routines but I feel as if it has not been noticed. I would like help but not much is explained to you in prison.

---

1. Nelson Mandela, *Long Walk to Freedom*, p.321

I have been here [for six months] and I haven't received any type of support from officers. I have felt that I have been disregarded as a human being and a prisoner.

It would be fair to say that some prisoners had received help and support. Peter said that

The opportunities are here if you want to take them.

Phil's experience had been quite positive.

Since I came here everyone supported me a lot. I didn't have any problems with anyone while I was here … Staff have been a lot of help to me to make my time in prison a bit easy.

Steven had also found help during his sentence and felt that he had been given a real opportunity to gain something from his sentence.

From the day I came here my caseworker has done everything possible to make sure I leave prison with as many things as possible to help me find employment and stop offending. I was even able to leave prison for a day to attend a college interview for when I leave here. I'm very pleased with the skills and qualifications that I have learned.

One comment suggests that the experience has been a mixed bag:

Well my comment is that the prison doesn't provide enough help for young people apart from the head of education. She do help to go out there and get people to introduce us to new activities but apart from providing other chances for young offenders such as doing activities, get out of their room doing things like that, they can do more for the young offenders if they provide the opportunity for us to get our minds off things that do affect us which lead to suicide and taking their life, etc. Provide young people, especially young offender, with more to do.

One of the elements of the prison regime, which has contributed to the prospects of rehabilitation and resettlement after release, is the prison education department. It seems that, in direct contrast to their very negative experiences of mainstream education, it can be one of the most important influences on changing behaviour. Comments from offenders in young offender institutions suggest that many have found salvation through education. This has not always been simply because it has provided them with skills and qualifications that will improve their prospects of employment but also because it has provided opportunities to reflect and to reconsider their own behaviour.

Ann Reuss described the impact of a sociology course she had taught to adult prisoners at HMP Full Sutton (Reuss 1999) from which it was clear that the opportunity to reflect on behaviour and to discuss consequences had been a significant influence on the thinking of the participants. The evaluation of a prison-based arts programme in Canada conducted by Duguid and Pawson (1998) also highlighted the impact that courses can have on individuals and on their rate of further offending. Many young offenders are not accessing courses at higher levels but still find value in the curriculum and the atmosphere of the education department. Their comments are indicative both of what prison might offer and also what that offer can cost.

As with many services in prison, education is subject to resource constraints and practical barriers to effective delivery. Education classes are not immediately available in every prison and for the more popular courses there will be a lengthy waiting list. Some young men had waited for over a month to access a course and while waiting had just been shut in their cells. Classes were also not available when there was a shortage of staff. This did not generally mean a shortage of teachers but more often too a shortage of prison staff to escort prisoners to lessons. Many of the young prisoners resented this not just because it disrupted education but also it meant staying locked in the cell without any notice or explanation. Increases in the prison population and reduced resources have made matters worse over the years.

Andrew was half way through his sentence and said,

> The whole jail has gone down. Officers are getting asked to do things one way, not the way they want to do it. They take it out on us. They say they haven't

got enough money. They keep looking for jobs and then they go. Classes get cancelled. You don't get told. Officers take us to classes late. That's time wasted.

Arif agreed with him:

The prison is understaffed and that puts pressure on education classes. You're only allowed so many a week. It's a problem of escorts. It's gone downhill with the amount going off sick and leaving for other jobs. It's difficult all round.

Steve was very positive about education but said,

Except when you get ready and it's cancelled because of lock down or because the teacher is sick. You never know what's happening every day. Worst is when it just gets cancelled.

Classes did get cancelled because a teacher was not available. John explained why it was such a problem when a class did not take place for any reason.

Worst when you're down for a class and the teacher don't show up. Then you're banged up till next day.

Classes had been cancelled and the range of subjects available reduced, because of lack of resources. There were also comments that the quality of materials in education was poor, again because of lack of resources. One comment from Lee was,

Not enough resources. For example we had to get information about businesses and you couldn't get up to date materials from the library.

Another comment demonstrates the age and quality of materials:

Books in classes are very old. There's an atlas dated 1963.

The broader prison system also had an impact. Jim was doing GCSEs while in custody and was moved from one prison a week before the exams. It meant that he was unable to take his exams. While prisoners may be moved because of disruptive behaviour it seemed more likely that, in his case, it was because of overcrowding and consequent prisoner movement.

One disadvantage to prison education has always been the wide range of age and ability within the group. Some of the youngest prisoners, some of whom were quite volatile, had difficulty in keeping still and concentrating for a whole session. They then misbehaved and that made it harder for the more serious students to concentrate. Leon was angry about the disruption, which made it harder for him to get on with his work.

People mess about. Prats mess about. Hard to concentrate.

Michael agreed with him, saying,

People mess about in class. Distract the teacher.

Despite the fact that other inmates provided distraction and interrupted classes these young men had not found that anyone tried to discourage them from taking part in education. In school there is often an issue, particularly for boys, that credibility goes with not working and not conforming but this seemed to be almost turned on its head in young offender institutions. Kelvin's comments help to explain why this should be so.

I was never interested in school, anyway people thought you were a prat if you did all the work and turned up to all the classes. Here it's different. You don't turn up, you're sitting in your cell all day. I'm in for a while this time. I'm going to get something out of the system while I'm here.

Research into experiences of adult education described by Ann Reuss in 1999 and Emma Hughes in 2000 suggests that older prisoners are discouraged from taking part in education by other inmates. Their research suggests a sense that to pursue any form of higher education is to be 'above your station', to be different from your peers and that this brings with it criticism, not only from other prisoners but also from prison staff. This did not seem to be so much of a concern for younger prisoners. This might be because they were in general involved in education at much lower levels but there also seemed to be a consensus that it was better to take part in education than to sit in a cell doing nothing. This also provided the excuse, should it be needed, for going to a class. It was always possible to say that it was just to get out of your cell or to gain privileges.

Education seemed to be very much part of the routine and for most it was much more than just getting out of the cell. Dave said that

...a lot of people take it seriously. No one thinks it's stupid to learn'.

Pete thought that even higher levels of education were acceptable within the prison culture. He said,

People have to do their own thing. The people that need to learn to read don't get mocked for that and it's the same at the other end of the spectrum.

Jamil agreed:

If someone is really making some achievement people are mature enough to respect that. If you're really trying people will help you.

Joe was taking a GNVQ and said,

Some people want to do it and they ask me about GNVQ. Some people don't care, they've got the same attitude they came in with. It makes me feel good that you've gained something and other people want to know about it.

It seems that while education in school has been something to kick against, education in prison has become almost an opportunity to demonstrate control over the system and to display increased maturity. It was the 'younger ones' or 'the stupid ones' who did not take part. They were the ones who still had the same old attitudes and they were the ones who would be coming back to jail. In these terms, education becomes the smart response to the situation. Learn new skills, get a job after release and don't end up back inside.

These young men had spoken in very negative terms about their school days and their relationship with teachers so there is clearly something different about education in prison, making it more acceptable. For most prisoners it is quite different. It is not compulsory. Class sizes are smaller so there is greater teacher attention and more understanding of poor concentration and disruptive behaviour. More teacher help was available because the class was smaller and the whole ethos was more relaxed and friendly. They also appreciated the fact that they were not treated like children.

Phil had not attended school very much and had found it boring. He had also struggled with some of the work when he did attend. He said that he had never had much help in school but he was now finding that he was beginning to learn new things.

> The environment is different. In school you're just given work to do. Here they give you a chance to catch up. Maths. I never thought I was any good at maths but you can just catch up.

Ben had been quite an able student at school but he had not got on well with the teachers. In school he said,

> I could sit at the back of the class and do nothing and get the work done in ten minutes at the end. They didn't like that. I couldn't sit there and be quiet for them.

He found the atmosphere in the prison education department different.

> You're treated more like an equal by the teachers. Those who say you aren't are the ones that mess around. If you're focused and working you're treated like an equal.

Leon said that in school teachers had not had much time for him.

> Some teachers if they saw you not working would say I don't have to teach you. I get paid anyway. Instead of giving some encouragement.

In prison he had found that

Teachers are more friendly. Smaller class more support. They don't tell you what to do, they don't force you. If you want to work they help you.

Jim also commented on a different attitude from the teachers.

It's loads different. Teachers don't expect you to be brainy. They say just do what you can.

As Alan summed it up,

School is childish. Here is grown up.

Many of these comments suggest that the education environment is different. Smaller classes, less formality, less pressure for examination success. In a prison the authority figures are the prison officers not the teachers and the more relaxed atmosphere clearly made students feel that they were treated with more respect. If this is the case it would suggest that prison education can offer the effective learning environment that Sammons et al (1995) described when they spoke of an environment in which the student was praised, encouraged and given opportunities to take responsibility for their own learning.

However, this is still a prison environment, with all that goes with it. For Jem, Robert and Naz the physical environment was oppressive.

Every time you look at the window you see bars.

You can't go outside. Just stand out in the hall for a break.

Not like school at all. No breathing space.

Learning to cope with the environment is not easy, especially for young men serving a first sentence. Gerard and Michael were very critical of the lack of explanation or of help with any problems.

> I don't think we get enough free flow or association. There isn't enough advice about what happens when you get released. Prison isn't easy and a bit confusing. There isn't enough information about what goes on. And once placed here you are advised to meet with prison rules even if you don't know what they are.

> Not to be funny but I think this prison is very badly run such as short staff et cetera so we do not have much time to talk to officers about our problems, as they are very busy. Not only is it unfair to inmates but also to staff.

For some, the atmosphere in the classroom was problematic. Ian found the less formal environment much too relaxed and was uncomfortable with the way that some students spoke to the staff. Euan suggested almost the reverse and described a tension in classes that made him feel uneasy.

> The way people talk. People swear. In school you had to respect the teacher.

> The atmosphere is different from school. I wouldn't say it's tense but in some groups you can cut the atmosphere with a knife.

Despite a more positive attitude towards education and learning it seems clear that it is not possible to ignore the fact that a YOI contains a large number of volatile young men in a confined environment.

For many of these young men they will not only have missed out on education itself but also the positive relationship with an adult that many children get from their teachers. There were many comments about teachers who were friendly and treated them with respect. Inevitably there were criticisms too. For some being too friendly was being too laissez-faire and allowing bad behaviour disruption in the class. But the relationship was often important and several young men commented on the fact that they were listened to.

Most of the young men commenting said that they thought education in prison had made a difference to them. For most this was expressed in terms of learning new skill, getting back into a way of working or providing something that will help with finding work on release. For example, Esten said,

It's helped me to get qualifications. Makes a difference if you put it all to use.

For Darren it helped him to reach a personal goal.

It's got me qualifications I've been after [them] a long time.

Even for the young men who had not yet achieved any qualifications there was a sense of progress for people like John.

When I was doing maths and that I wasn't good at it. Now I can count and I know what I'm doing. It has helped.

There was also acknowledgement that the achievement was only possible because of the time spent in custody. As Darren said,

Getting an NVQ. Wouldn't have had the motivation on the out.

For some of the young men there had been little impact. Some were not sure it would make a difference after release while others felt that any improvements were down to their own efforts. Paul said,

No I've improved my writing. Taught myself. Not education.

Adam's comment highlights a view that a decision to change is a personal one and that courses run by the prison could have little impact.

I know why I'm inside and what I did was wrong so learning about victim awareness is pointless. Courses can't change me. Only I can do it.

One of the younger men was quite open about the fact that he intended to return to crime and he saw no benefit at all in education or any other programme that the prison could provide.

For the most part it was those who had already gained qualifications who did not think that prison education would make any difference to them. Sometimes because they were already committed to education but others because education in prison could not offer them enough. David had been taking A-levels at the time of his arrest and said it would not help him.

> Not at the present level. Might do something more challenging later on.

In contrast there were many comments from young men who spoke of the impact of education in prison not just in terms of their skill development and employability but also on their thinking, their confidence and their attitude.

A series of very brief comments all suggest that there has been some time to reflect and to think about a different way of life. Some of these young men had been in prison for some time so that they were significantly older than they had been when they last offended but there was also a sense that something, during their sentence, had acted as something of a catalyst:

> Could help me live my life differently.

> I'm taking more of an interest in myself.

> Made me realise things. I've grown up.

> It has definitely. If it wasn't all of my thinking would be as it was before. It's saved me in a way.

> Its made me think.

> I see life differently. People say I'm more mature.

> Made me realise there's more in life.

Some of the comments indicate regret about school and acceptance of responsibility for their behaviour there. Pete thought that

> The best thing about school is learning but I didn't see that. Didn't want to see it. Kids don't want to do things. Later you realise you've made a mistake.

While for some the distance may have lent enchantment to the view, there was a real sense that school had been a time of opportunity and that that opportunity had been wasted. Many took responsibility for their actions and accepted that they had contributed to the negative experience that school had been.

Majid acknowledged that he had wasted opportunities because of his behaviour:

I was anti-authority. I was dumb, young, never realistic.

Pete recognized that he had been out of control:

I was wild at the time.

Andrew and Jamie and Jason all accepted that they had not behaved well.

Thought I was too good for the place.

I made a real mess of it.

I had behaviour problems. I was in the wrong crowd.

The increased maturity will not be solely due to experiences in prison education. Some of the young men commenting are older and, therefore more mature in their thinking. Some of them had taken part in other activities and programmes. The cognitive skills courses that some had undertaken will have had some impact on their attitude. There had been changes in their circumstances outside of prison. One of the young men had become a father since the start of his sentence. Some felt that it was the sentence itself that had made a difference to them, especially those who were serving a longer one. This was true for Ross, who was serving a three year sentence.

I'm working my butt off to get qualifications. When I came to jail for a long time I realised it is better to get something out of it. You do it because you want to.

Most of these young men spoke of plans for the future, which should not have been unrealistic or unattainable. Dan, for example, had plans for higher education.

> Move to London and I should start college. If, in August, I've passed psychology and criminology I stand a good chance of getting in to college to get a diploma. I also want to do A-level sport and recreation. Then I want to go to university.

Leon explained that, having had time to think things through, he could see where he had gone wrong and could see what he needed to do while in prison to have more of a chance in life after his release.

> I looked at me life. When I was at school I made a real mess of it. I want to see if I can get a few qualifications. Make a fresh start. With qualifications I'll have something to show whereas before I had nothing to show at a job interview.

Colin's options were more limited. He had badly injured his leg in a motorbike accident and was clearly torn between finding ways to mange alone or relying on his mother.

> I'd like to work from home. I'm registered disabled because of my leg so I'm stranded really. My mum runs a pub and I could work for her again but I'd rather go alone.

Shaw had no choice but to go it alone.

> First a bed sit. I was with a girl and she was sorting it but we've split now so I've got to find somewhere.

Steve also had limited options. He was going back to live with his mother but had begun to realise that he could not rely on her indefinitely.

> I had mental health problems before. They said I was a something path, not psychopath but if my mother needs the money I'll work.

Jonathan had also had mental health issues. His parents had been extremely supportive throughout his sentence and they recognised that he would always need some additional support in his life.

> Will go back to live with my parents. I've got the support of my family so I'm luckier than most.

For many young offenders the possibility of further education is very closely related to lifestyle change and a move away from crime as all of these brief comments suggest:

> Will apply to college when released.

> College and a part time job.

> I want to do drama classes.

> Going back to college.

> College in September to do A-levels.

> Back to college to do electronic engineering. A lot of my family work with cable TV. I'm interested in that.

Joe has some very clear ideas about future career prospects and was planning to get the qualifications and experience to put his plans into action.

> Finish my technicians certificate. Then I need work experience and then I get the exam from Toyota. I want to open a garage, specialise in gear boxes. Electronics and gear boxes is where the money is. I'm going to talk to the Prince's Trust.

Anwar also had employment plans:

> Drama. I've been told they want Asian actors. I like taking risks but not criminal any more. I can make anyone laugh. I make them laugh in here.

Some young men spoke of settling down, of wanting a home and family. Keith was already a father and said,

> I just want to get back to see the bairn. I've hardly seen him.

Others were grimly determined to be independent, like Craig.

> I'm never on the dole. I don't live with my parents. I have to be independent, look after myself. I'll find something. See what's around.

Most of the plans were about a home, education, a job, a family and, sometimes, just staying out of trouble and out of prison. Carl just wanted 'To stay out of trouble'. Arif explained more fully why he wanted to change:

> Prison makes a difference to you. You lose your freedom. I'm not coming back. I'm going to stay out of trouble. I've got better things to do than coming in here.

These were young men expressing a wish for the same things that other young men of the same age might wish for. Stability, employment, a relationship, family and an independent life. The risk for them is that their background and their offending will deny them even these relatively basic desires. Their lifestyle choice would appear to be a pretty standard law-abiding one. The problem is that there are barriers to these ambitions and to making these choices.

This is not an argument for being 'soft on crime'. These are young men who, for the most part, accept that their behaviour has been wrong. They understand that there has been a reason for punishment and they have done their time. Now they need an opportunity to move on. It is well known that young offenders leaving custody are often seduced back into crime within a very short time. There are a number of possible reasons, even for those who are genuinely committed to change. Dealers wait at the nearest station for the young men who have been released that day. They are easily identifiable as they carry their possessions in the standard issue bag. Friends wait at the gate. Sometimes it is well-intentioned, though the celebratory drinking session sometimes proves to be a mistake. Sometimes they are there to involve the young man in another crime. Sometimes there is nobody waiting and prison staff have spoken of young men who walk out of the gate and don't even know whether to turn left or right. The first few days after leaving prison are intensely traumatic. There will be statutory support for the young offender but this is about compliance with licence conditions rather than about practical help and moral support. Indeed, some offenders will say that the licence arrangements are as much in the way of going straight as they are a mechanism for helping. A prisoner in one establishment was back inside because of a breach of his licence conditions. He had not committed any further offences so his return to custody was solely because of non-compliance. He was very angry about it and said,

> I had got a job and I had got a place to live. There was room there for my kid to come and see me. It was all great. I missed appointments with the probation officer. I was at work. I should have let her know I couldn't get there but there you go. For that I am back inside and I am going to have to start all over again when I get out. The licence sets you up to fail.

The provision of services for offenders after release from custody is often contentious. There are frequent objections to providing housing for offenders, especially in areas where housing is difficult to come by for non-offenders too. There are arguments against providing support for the most vulnerable prisoners on the same basis; why should people who have done something wrong have access to something not available to the law-abiding?

The response is twofold. First why should there not be support services in place for people who need them, whether they are offenders or not? Secondly, this is not simply about the individual offender, it is also about reducing crime and the potential of victims of crime. Life after release is hard for most prisoners and, finding it so hard, they are likely to relapse. If support and assistance reduces that risk, it must surely better for all of us. One prison governor described work on resettlement and rehabilitation in his prison as a means of 'preventing the next victim'.

Offenders themselves have a range of suggestions about the help that is needed if those that want to change are to have the opportunity to do so.

Tony's comments highlight a common problem for young offenders. Finding somewhere to live is doubly difficult if there are arrears owing on previous accommodation. This creates a Catch 22 situation. It is very difficult to find work if you have no address then how do you find the money to pay off the arrears so that it is possible to find somewhere to live?

> I would like to see somebody about everything while I'm in prison because I could use the help from people in prison and when I get released from the prison because I have nowhere to live and I need to get a job to pay my rent off at the other hostel I lived at before I got put in prison.

Several of the young men pointed to shortcomings in the prison and the lack of help and support available, especially for some of the most vulnerable prisoners. Matt accepted that there had been some improvements in regimes but still pointed out failures in the system.

> I think the Prison Service has improved but it still has a long way to go in improving the chances of finding work or a training course on discharge, on bullying and discrimination and making use of a sentence while in prison. The worst thing I have found is there is no help for the mentally disturbed and handicapped. There is no easy access to a psychologist unless a doctor says it is possible to see one and I don't think doctors are trained whether to make that decision.

David said, 'I think there should be more home visits.' Home visits, town visits and opportunities to be back in the community prior to release have all proved helpful in the resettlement process.

For both Martin and Mick there was a real need for support both during and after sentence, both realised that they were likely to have great difficulty in coping alone.

> I am hoping to get a drug treatment and testing order (DTTO) programme when I get out. I have been in prison a few times and go back to drugs when I get out because I'm either homeless when I get out or there is no-one to help me stay away from drugs. As you can appreciate it is very hard to stay away from crack and heroin and I admit to myself I need help and want help.

I would like to have an allocated worker for my depression and self-harming because it keeps running me down and I don't think I'll be able to cope much longer.

There are several practical points that would make it easier to find work and to find somewhere to live. Ian's suggestion reflects a concern expressed by many young men. It is likely to be much harder to find work while it is necessary to disclose a criminal record. He is not suggesting that there should be no disclosure but rather that the existing periods for disclosure are too long.

People should be helped to get back into society by having shorter disclosure periods.

Perhaps the need to disclose would be less of a problem if Ian's suggestion were to be taken up. There is clearly a great deal of prejudice against young people with a criminal record, despite the fact that, often, an employee with a record will have a major contribution to make to the employer's business. Jem suggested that work should be done to

Break down prejudice from employers.

Phil provides one of the reasons why employment can be so important.

Help with employment is important. Then you're not on the streets because you've got to get up and go to work in the morning. Even if you are offered a job it takes time to get into the regime. I was a bad lad on the booze but you don't listen when you're drinking.

Jed's comments endorse his view:

Kids have got to try and stay out of trouble. Working kept me out of trouble. This gives you something to get up for so you don't stay out so late. People drink 24/7 and you can't if you've got somewhere to go.

Andy's comment also helps to demonstrate that employment is not just about having income. It is also about having structure and occupation during the day.

> I started drinking every day. Now I drink less. I feel better and I got into trouble when I was drinking. Need something to do all day. When there is nothing to do people are at risk.

Pete summed up the view of many of the young men that getting qualifications and increasing the chances of getting work would help in reducing the risk of offending:

> Getting qualifications. Education and a job stop you getting into trouble.

It is, of course, not just employment that makes a difference , as Leon said;

> Seven out of ten prisoners with a place to live and the chance to get a job would not re-offend.

When Steve was asked what he thought agencies could do to help his response was:

> Making sure people have a roof over their heads.

A decent roof over his head would have satisfied Phil who said that what he needed was 'A stable home'. Pete agreed with that but also saw the need for managing drug addictions.

> Safe, stable accommodation and legal prescription drugs so they don't need to steal.

One of the problems for many young offenders is accessing services. They are often not skilled in explaining their needs and many have commented that the response that they get from agencies that might help them is poor.

Andy recognised that very basic help might make it easier for young offenders to get the help that they need.

> Help with filling out forms and advocacy with agencies.

One comment from Arif comes right back to the notion of life choices and the very real perception that young offenders do not have many options available to them nor opportunities to make positive choices.

> Offering more options … to choose in life.

A number of the young offenders making comments were being housed in projects run by the voluntary sector, where they were provided with both a roof over their head and with a great deal of support. This gave many of them an opportunity to reflect on their own lives and to take time, in a safe environment, to think about where they might go next. Jim said that what had helped him was,

> Having the space to be honest with myself.

Dave said that he had learned,

> To look after myself. Go to the doctor.

For Peter it had

> Helped [me] to gain confidence.

The physical environment was also much appreciated.
Julian was knocked out by the accommodation he was offered.

> It's brilliant. I was homeless and living on the streets before. I was gob-smacked at how nice the properties are. It's been a breath of fresh air.

But it is about more than the physical environment. For Jimmy it was about the help and the listening ear that he was offered.

> The staff are really good. Whatever help I need whether it's just to talk or to look into things like college they can help.

Gerry welcomed

> Being involved; made to feel a part of the service. Being valued as an individual.

For Ian, as well, the attitude of the staff was important.

> People who are nice and welcoming.

When so many young offenders comment on being treated by people in authority with hostility and without respect it is understandable that this should be something to highlight.

One of the most poignant comments came from Mark. He had been living on the streets for some time. Asked what was the best thing about the project he replied, 'Feeling safe'.

Having the help had given many of the young men the impetus to think more about themselves so that Dan thought the best thing for him had been

> Learning things about the consequences of your actions.

On the practical side, Euan said,

> Before I wasn't good at paying bills but now I'm on top of that.

Peter said,

> I can cook, know where the library is and the council offices. Know how to use them. Got the practical skills to keep the flat together. In a safe bubble but not taking anything for granted.

Many of the projects were seen as places that were

Helping people who want to get their lives sorted.

Help and advice and 'someone you can trust, someone to talk to' were seen to be very important and so there was considerable support for the idea of mentoring. There are many examples of mentoring projects aimed at prisoners during their sentence and following their release. It has been seen by many as a sensible means of making sure that offenders are able to access the services they need. The impact for some individuals has been overwhelming. Karl spoke about his mentor:

If I ever offend again I'll probably feel ashamed about it this time. All the other times when I come into prison this time I didn't really care about no-one. I just thought when I get out I'll do the same thing over and over again. But he's helped me through that, got me off the pattern of getting out and committing crimes and coming back in again. Hopefully I'll be able to sort myself out.

Several young men provided examples of support, which had helped them get access to services that they desperately needed. One example was a young man who needed to claim benefit and make his claim as a matter of urgency. He went with his support worker to the benefits office where they waited for three hours. He was treated quite rudely and dismissively by staff and it was only because the support worker intervened that the claim was made and his basic income assured. He said afterwards.

It was only because she was there. I never would have waited all that time on me own. I'd have lost it and walked out.

Walking out would have left him without any immediate prospect of legitimate income and a much increased risk of stealing to buy food.

Someone who acts as an advocate or intermediary is often of great value. There were a number of cases where the young person received shabby treatment at housing offices, GP's surgeries and benefits offices. They were aware that their own responses might have been aggressive and it is likely that their reactions to the people in authority would have provoked the same hostility that had earlier drawn reactions from teachers or police officers. A responsible adult able to diffuse a potentially hostile situation, to provide a clear explanation of what was required and willing to stay with the young person until any problems were resolved had made a significant difference. Craig explained what had happened to him:

> I was on this training scheme and I was at home but then I had this big row with my dad and I got thrown out. I didn't know what to do. I turned up at the centre with all my stuff in bags and said I had nowhere to go. The boss came with me to the housing place. I was so pleased she was there. At first this woman just told me off and she was saying it was all my fault that I hadn't got anywhere to live. So the boss said that this wasn't right and I had to have somewhere to go. They found me something for the night. It wasn't great but better than nothing. I wouldn't have got anything at all if she wasn't there. The housing weren't gonna help me.

Rees also commented on the difference it had made just to have someone with him:

> It makes a difference if someone goes with you. I've been to all these offices and things before and they just treat you like shit. It's much better with someone there. Moral support like.

There were also many comments about the value of having someone who would listen, might challenge what the young person said but would demonstrate that they cared what happened. John described the relationship he had with his mentor:

> He used to come from miles away to see me when I was still inside. He didn't have to do that. He doesn't get paid to do it even. He just does it. Now I'm out we keep in touch. We meet up and I talk to him about what is going on. He was great at first. He talked to my parents and then they let me stay there for a bit. Then he helped me with my own place. Even came shopping with me so I knew what stuff to get. It was brilliant. I've been out a while now and I'm doing okay. We still meet up sometimes. Sometimes we just text. I sent a text when I got me

job. He sent back saying well done and he was proud of me. No-one had ever said they was proud of me before. I don't want to get into any more trouble anyway but now I don't want to let him down.

The idea of offering support was also a two way street. Several offenders wanted the opportunity to talk to other young people, to discourage them from getting involved in crime or with drugs. A group of young people at a project for recovering drug addicts discussed ways in which they could help other young people who came into contact with drugs:

Resettlement programmes could send people to talk to young people and get them to meet real people with experiences of getting into trouble or going through the system.

Drop in centre. Talking to each other. Support for each other.

Peer support. Mentors. Buddies. Any time of day or night.

Several young people said that they thought that ex-offenders would have a lot to offer to young people on the periphery of crime and to young people who had been through the system and wanted to get out of it.

They know what it's like. They've been there. They know when it's hard.

Certainly the examples of former gang members working to keep other young people away from gangs has demonstrated the effectiveness of this approach.

There was also a sense that ex-offenders would have a good idea about those who really wanted help and those who were playing the system. Dave said,

To use support appropriately and get the most out of it, it has to be worked at.

There was also a sense of take it or leave it when it came to providing help, recognising that not everyone who seeks the support is ready to change.

Doug said, 'There are two roads. You take one or the other.' Joe agreed and suggested that you can only point someone in the right direction, 'Can give them a path. If they screw up they do'.

Tony pointed to the importance of a personal commitment. Personal decision. 'Depends on the person. If they want to they will'.

Adam also recognised the need to take personal responsibility but also the amount of help that was available to him through the project if he was prepared to try.

> If you put in the effort they'll do anything for you here.

There was a strong consensus about this personal choice. Inevitably there will be people who are offered support and who reject or abuse it. There will be people who do want to change but who, even with help, find it difficult or impossible. Help in finding a home or a job is only a first step in any case. You have to keep it. Learning how to manage budgets, develop a work ethic, pay the rent, avoid the loud parties or the dealing from the premises is, or should be, part and parcel of resettlement and rehabilitation. Sometimes it will seem that the best efforts to help have been wasted. Sometimes, though, it is just that it takes a while for it all to come together.

Noel was a classic example. He talked about his experience after his release from prison:

> I really did have it all on a plate. I had a job to go to and I had a reasonable place to live. I also had a mentor who was a really good bloke. I didn't do too badly at first but then I started getting into a bit of debt and I did a bit of nicking, to try to make ends meet. I don't know if it was because I was worried about that but I started to piss about at work. I was late a lot and sometimes I didn't turn up and when I did I was looking at porn on the computer. Of course I got the push. Then I couldn't pay the rent and it just all went downhill. My mentor was still trying to help me. He was telling me that I could get it all together. He told me that he was sure I had what it takes to succeed. I wasn't really listening at the time. I got picked up again and did another sentence. Funnily enough I didn't have all the same chances when I came out that time but I guess I was a bit older and also I met this girl. We got a place together and I got a job pretty soon after

I came out. Long story short. I'm married now and we've got a kid. I'm working and we've got a decent place. I think that maybe two years ago I just wasn't in the mind set to be any different but I did remember the things that he said to me. Now I can't see me ever getting into trouble again. I rang my old mentor. Told him that all that he said to me had finally sunk in. Told him about the job and the kid. He was chuffed.

CHAPTER SIX

A CHANCE OF SUCCESS BY DOING THINGS DIFFERENTLY

To know all makes one tolerant.

Mme. De Sael, *Corinne*, 1807

Happy he, who could understand the causes of things.

Virgil, *Aeneid*

The consequence of our existing approach to dealing with young people who are anti-social and who commit crimes is that there are a lot of young men, some little more than children, who are in prison. There is a school of thought that would say that is quite right. We have heard often enough demands to 'Lock them up and throw away the key'. It is often a response to crime made by people who are not in possession of all the facts, who have no experience of prison and no reason to be aware of the circumstances that may lead to the commission of a crime and the receipt of a prison sentence. Often it is a wish expressed by those who do not know what they wish for. Do we really want to use a prison system that is vastly expensive, is a major cost to the tax payer, that may do more to increase the risk of further crime than to diminish the risk and which is often ineffective in reducing offending by young people? Would we want, knowing what it is like to be in prison, to have children and young people kept in such an institution?

Although the number of young men in custody had fallen during 2010 there are still significant numbers who experience life in a young offender institution. There may be some debate about whether all of those young people should be in custody but the fact remains that it will be a reality for some. Custody should be a last resort, not least because, however constructive the regime, loss of liberty and confinement have damaging consequences. Both Vivien Stern in 1998 and Angela Neustatter in 2002 commented that the impact of custody on young people is rarely entirely beneficial and is all too often tragic. Young men are bullied and stigmatised. They harm them-selves and some commit suicide. Evidence suggests that there is a high risk of becoming institutionalised even after a relatively short sentence and there are obvious limitations on anything approaching a normal life when the perimeter is a fence or wall topped with wire. If boys in general, and young offenders in particular, are likely to be physically active and boisterous then the vision of several hundred volatile young men confined within a relatively small area is a daunting one.

It is possible for the prison regime to offer opportunity. Martin Narey, when he was Director General of HM Prison Service, spoke of the posi-tive aspects of the juvenile regime (Howard League Conference, 2001). He pointed out that custody is not disrupting the lives of these young people. There lives were chaotic and disrupted before they came into the prison. Becoming a captive audience provides opportunities for them to enjoy some stability and structure and to learn new skills. David Wilson (2002) in argu-ing that prison education can have a beneficial impact says,

> You can't ignore the fact that they are physically active, often bored, and prison education departments can be a welcome diversion for those having a hard time. If teachers can capitalise on this and treat prisoners as individuals and with kind-ness they may be able to lead inmates to see that they can enjoy education.

Both of the above statements may be regarded as examples of the way in which help can be provided within a secure environment but it is a damn-ing indictment of the way in which a society is prepared to treat some of its children. Instead of helping them and giving them opportunities to change there are perceived advantages to locking them up in an environment which the then Chief Inspector of Prisons, Sir (now Lord) David Ramsbotham, described as 'brutalising and inhumane'. In an inspection of one YOI in 2003, another chief inspector, Ann Owers (Now Dame Ann Owers), was highly critical of the atmosphere of the place and commented that many of the juveniles were afraid to leave their cells. However positive a prison regime may be it is essential that we should not forget that this is an envi-ronment in which some young people are quite unable to cope. Writing in 1998 Vivien Stern said,

Visiting prisons is a sad business. But the saddest aspect is seeing the young people, the 15, 16 and 17-year-old boys. They have a cheeky bravado, which often cloaks terror or despair. They have a hollow-eyed haunted look.

Fear, violence and bullying are endemic in prisons. This is a not unnatural consequence of confining large groups of young men, some of them vulnerable, some of them disturbed, in a locked institution where there is little opportunity for physical activity and even less for privacy. Goffman (1968) in describing prisons as 'total institutions' commented on the unnatural state in which prisoners find themselves, confined in the same place and with the same people. He suggested that many prisoners are able to adjust to the environment and, indeed, have to adjust in order to survive. The consequence, however, is frequently an inability to cope with the world outside after the period of confinement. Former prisoners often describe a lack of confidence in social situations and difficulty in re-establishing relationships. One prisoner explained,

> You don't have any common ground to talk to anyone else. When you first meet people they'll talk about their job or where they went on holiday last year or what they did for Christmas. What can I say?

When Pete went home after his sentence he found that things were very different to the way they had been before.

> It was all different. I just thought she don't need me here any more. She just did everything. I know she had to while I was inside but it was as if there was nothing I could do. She didn't need me at all.

An older prisoner, released after a long sentence, described his feelings after release:

> It was beyond imagination for me. Everything was different. I went to get on the bus and the stop wasn't there any more. It was so busy in the town. Loud and people drive so quick. I kept getting lost and then I felt a fool. I grew up in the place so how could I get lost?

Institutionalised , alienated, unable to find work and unable to get somewhere suitable to live we face a real risk of creating an underclass; a society of dispossessed young people who have never had, and perhaps never will have much of a chance in life. It is understandable that victims and communities should seek some redress for crimes committed against them but the retribution sought seems strangely disproportionate.

Society in the United Kingdom tends, on the face of it, to be punitive. The response to misdemeanours among young people tends to involve punishment and there is an emphasis on punishment first, even when there is a subsequent rehabilitative element. It is essentially a criminal justice model for dealing with crime. The evidence, however, would suggest that the commission of crime is merely a symptom of other more entrenched problems. The alternative is an approach, which looks at the history behind the crime and seeks to eradicate problems in the history and in the environment, not just for an individual but for children and young people more generally. In the current climate this is an extremely contentious argument. It is unlikely that there will be much public support for such an approach when, it would appear, the British public still want young people not to be seen and not to be heard either, where young people are not given much respect and where there is a perception that youth crime is spiralling out of control. It is that perception and the fears it brings which lead to such a punitive approach.

Despite statistics and research there remains a disproportionate fear of crime in British society. While a large proportion of the population believes that they are seriously at risk of becoming a victim of crime it is unlikely that there will be support for doing anything that appears to be less rigorous in dealing with crime. This suggests that any change in the approach to dealing with youth crime must go hand in hand with strategies to change public perceptions, to reduce the fear of crime and to restore confidence in the ability of any justice system, or any alternative to the justice model, to deal with crime.

Change there must be if we are not to continue to treat our young people with hostility and suspicion and if we are to tackle crime effectively. It is significant that many young people, not exclusively young offenders, speak of the negative way they are treated by adults. The hostility towards young people on the streets for example, or the level of service they receive in shops. Young offenders comment on the way in which they are spoken to by teachers, police officers or prison staff. Young black men commenting on the number of times that they were stopped and searched were generally philosophical about the fact of being stopped. What made them angry was the way in which they were treated, in some police areas, when they were stopped. Equally they speak positively and appreciatively about teachers in prison, mentors and key workers who have listened to them and have treated them like responsible and valuable young adults.

There is a great deal of evidence about the causes of crime and what works in preventing it but this is only likely to be acted upon if there is a strong political will to do so. There are examples of the impact of that strong will. In the early part of the 20th-century, the prison population was dramatically reduced. This might be explained by the fact that members of the government had direct experience of the impact of imprisonment. Women involved in the suffragette movement had been imprisoned and experienced brutal treatment. Winston Churchill had been a prisoner of war. He understood what it means to lose liberty and was determined that this should only be an act of last resort. There has rarely been that political will again. Instead, for many years, the political parties have sought to 'out tough' each other. No Home Secretary or Minister of Justice has wanted to be seen as the one who was soft on crime. It is perhaps ironic that we now have a different reason for greater political will to reduce the use of custody; an economic one.

Despite the fear of crime and despite a very high prison population most people know comparatively little about crime and punishment. They may hear second hand or read in the newspaper about life in a prison but, thankfully, relatively few will have reason to visit a prison and to see the environment and the inmates at first hand. Many people may hear about a serious crime and the consequent punishment but very few would ever have access to all the details about the circumstances of the offence or the background of the perpetrator. It is an interesting phenomenon to watch someone who has had no experience of prisons visit a prison, especially one holding young offenders, for the first time. Seeing the inside of a prison with the noise and the smells and the real sense of loss of liberty is an eye opening experience for the uninitiated. Seeing the inmates is similarly eye opening. Vivien Stern's comments are not exaggeration. Often young prisoners are undersized and vulnerable, full of a desperate bravado but, none the less, scared of what will happen in the prison and what will come after. One of the benefits of involving volunteers to work with young offenders both in prison and on the outside, has been the raising of awareness about who these young people are. Knowing the person, knowing the facts tends to lead to a less punitive and more thoughtful approach.

There have been some interesting experiments where groups of people, not associated with the criminal justice system, have been asked to say what they think the punishment should be in a series of ostensibly hypothetical cases. Once they have all the information that is available the general trend is to opt for a sentence that is less punitive than the sentence that was actually imposed. This would suggest that people are less punitive than we are led to believe, and indeed they are led to believe. The tabloid press would have us understand that the public are 'baying for blood' and want the most severe penalties to be imposed. The reality is usually that what is wanted is for a particular crime to stop. The important thing is that it does not happen again. And even the tabloid press appears to support treatment for drug users rather than punishment, recognising the need to deal with the real problem rather than the crime, which may be a symptom of it.

One of the dangers of the limited information and the way in which it is presented is the confusion of all sorts of crime and criminals. Of course it is right that the serial killer, the professional criminal, the serious and violent offender should receive a severe punishment. There are some crimes where only the most severe penalties could serve. But these are not the most common offenders. These are not the people who are speaking in this book. These are the vulnerable, the disadvantaged and the weak. Some of them may have done things that are unacceptable but this will often have been a symptom of what has gone before.

Crime and anti-social behaviour must be dealt with. That is not questioned in this book. It is the 'how' which is up for questioning. What is needed is a radical re-think of the way in which youth crime and young people are treated. The arguments for the need to change are moral, practical and economic.

The cost of the prison estate is immense. At a time of economic constraint and cutbacks it is harder than ever to justify the billions spent on locking people up. It may well be that economic constraints will help to win the argument with the public, media and politicians alike that we need to do something different. However, it is unacceptable and unrealistic to talk of reducing the prison population if there are people who genuinely have to be in a secure environment for a period of time. While we can argue that there are people in custody who do not need to be there, because they do not represent a danger to the public and, or because their imprisonment is likely to do more harm than good, we cannot ignore the proportion of prisoners who do need to be incarcerated because they do present a danger to the public or because their behaviour is so entrenched and persistent that sentencers are left with little choice but to impose a custodial sanction. Reducing the prison population has to start much further back, by investing in those factors that reduce crime in the first place or reduce the escalation of petty crime into something else. In order to do that we must first find ways to put young people and crime into a sensible perspective.

Rutherford's spectrum of offending is a useful device for putting crime into perspective. If there is a change in approach at the lower end of the spectrum there is a real opportunity to keep some young people out of crime, a further group out of the criminal justice system and a further group out of custody. At every point in the spectrum there is more that could be done to keep young people out of crime and out of the system. At worst, there is much more that could be done to help those young people who have become involved in the system, to get out of it again. It is especially important that we focus more attention at the lower end of the spectrum. Not because we should write off even the most serious offender, there may be change in even the most hardened criminal, but because for young people we are describing mistakes made before they are adult that may affect them throughout their adult lives.

Sweden and other Scandinavian countries focus attention on primary prevention; preventing young people from getting involved in crime in the first place. The age of criminal responsibility is much higher than that in the UK so that the attention is actually on the family. There is widespread evidence that the family, and its success or failure as a supportive and cohesive unit, has immense impact on offending behaviour. Graham and Bowling (1995) comment:

In sum, therefore, it would appear that the quality of family relationships and the closeness of parental supervision constitute important explanations for a range of problems that arise during adolescence, including truancy from school, contact with delinquent peers and offending itself. Once these factors are taken account of, social class and family size have no significant relationship with offending, whilst family structure remains indirectly related to offending through its influence on the capacity of parents to build and maintain good relationships with their children and to carefully supervise where and with whom they spend their time outside the home.

This would argue the case for interventions and support mechanisms that are designed to build the capacity of parents. It also implies that such support mechanisms are genuinely accessible to the parents who most need them. It further implies that the provision should be through a welfare model rather than a criminal justice model. The use of a criminal justice system to regulate the quality of parenting sits oddly with the need for children to learn how to socialise and to respect the norms of a community. A punishment model relies on the notion of some unpleasant consequence to the individual should they do something wrong, but it is clearly more desirable to discourage the possibility of wrongdoing by developing, in the individual, respect and concern for others so that they understand that it is not acceptable to behave in an anti-social way. This is a model which is likely to be effective for families and children where there is an intention to 'do right' though there may be constraints on their ability to do it.

It has already been acknowledged that there are children and families where that intention is not apparent. The likelihood then is that the children of the family will be at greater risk of offending and in order to address this there must be resources for agencies, not criminal justice agencies, to intervene and to provide the support that the parents have not provided.

Support for families and individual support for young people themselves could combine to keep significant numbers of young people out of the criminal justice system altogether. It will never be the case that all young people will avoid offending or can be kept out of the system. What it would mean would be a reduced risk of that early involvement in crime, which escalates to a point where custody becomes the only option. It would reduce the prison population so that only those who must be in custody are in custody and resources could be spent on providing a constructive and rehabilitative regime designed to reduce the risks of re-offending on release for that smaller number of prisoners.

All the evidence seems to point to the family as the significant starting point and that would suggest that this is the place for urgent investment. The concept of early intervention is not new. It is generally accepted that trying to influence the thinking and the actions of a small child are considerably easier than trying to influence an adolescent or an adult. At the start of 2011 two new pieces of literature supported the need to act early. In her book *Couch Fiction*, Philippa Perry argues the importance of stimulus to promote brain development after birth. Pathways are developed in relationship with our earliest caregivers, and, if the relationship with the early care givers is less than ideal it is likely to lead to emotional difficulties. Graham Allen produced a government commissioned report into early intervention programmes for young people. His report focuses on the first three years of a child's life when, he argues, 'We see the most explosive bit of brain growth'. His contention is that investment at that stage is far more effective than intervention at a later stage. It is also, he points out, much cheaper.

Add up the costs of all the late interventions, all the remedial work, reading recovery, special needs teaching, schemes for job readiness, teenage pregnancy, drink and drug abuse, a lifetime on benefits.

But early intervention itself has also had some bad press. There are two significant reasons. One is that early intervention via a criminal justice route is not only unlikely to help but may make matters far worse (McCara and McVie 2007). Evidence suggests that labelling young people as offenders is likely to increase the risk of further offending. The other is that predictors of offending are not 100% reliable. They may be strongly indicative and they may point to increased risk but it cannot be assumed that there is an inevitability about offending just because a young man comes from a broken home in a city slum area. In addition, while there are obvious links between early stimulus and brain development, Walsh (2010) points to the dangers of using neuroscience as a predictor of future criminality. These provisos point to an argument that what is vitally important is the early assessment of the situation. They suggest that the early involvement should not be through criminal justice, nor should it be because there is a fear that a child may become an offender. It should happen because there is a child who may be in need and whose needs are not being met.

Most of the early risk indicators should be identified by health professionals, by carers or by teachers, the people who are most likely to come into contact with the child. Midwives visit babies and young mothers in their homes. It should be possible, given sufficient time and resources, to see whether the child and mother are thriving. Is the baby clean and dry? Are there other children in the house who look uncared for? Is the child picked up and spoken to? This is not about identifying child abuse but about getting a sense of whether the mother is coping, whether there is any post natal depression, whether there is financial hardship. Essentially it is about looking to offer support where that may be needed, not looking to blame or criticise. Involvement and intervention needs to be about providing support when it is needed, not about leaving parents in fear that their children will be taken away from them.

If we can describe a spectrum of offending perhaps there is also a spectrum for family support and childcare. At one end there will be families who cope well and who give their children the level of support that they need. They may not be wealthy, they may indeed have very limited resources but they can offer a loving home and will pay attention to their children in every way. Generally they would require no particular intervention or additional help.

Then there will be families who would normally cope but are not able to do so temporarily. This might be because of some trauma; bereavement, redundancy, a difficult birth. It should be possible for those families to access additional support for the time that they need it.

There will also be families who are never able to cope well. They may wish to but they will probably always need some level of support. It is important that society recognises that there will always be some individuals and families who will never cope with independent living without access to substantial support. This can be because of mental health issues or a lack of education and good parenting in their own lives, which means that they have little understanding of what needs to be done to care adequately for the children.

At the far end of the spectrum there will be families who don't care for their children. This is where children are neglected or abused and where there is a more urgent need for intervention. These are the children who may need to be looked after outside of the family.

Across the country there are examples of family support projects and mentoring services that are designed to help families who want to cope but are not able to do so. There is a cost, of course, in providing that resource but it is a fraction of the cost of a child who has not been looked after getting seriously ill or becoming an offender. If it is not always possible to provide the support a child needs through the family there is a further potential for remedial help in the school situation.

There is huge potential for teachers to identify children who have difficulties and help to address them. In recent times there has been an increase in awareness of the child who stammers because of the film 'The Kings Speech'. A writer who was himself a stammerer writing in the *Guardian* commented that he had spoken to teachers who said that they had never taught a child who stammered. He found this unlikely. What was more likely was that the child had learned to hide it, usually by being very quiet in class. Devlin points to older prisoners who remember problems in school because they could not read the board or could not hear what the teacher said. She suggests that these are not uncommon examples of undiagnosed disability. Prisoners involved in research carried out by Edinburgh University were angry as only because of this research had they been diagnosed as dyslexic. Not only had they struggled in school because of their dyslexia but they had been told off for not writing and spelling properly. There is a resource issue in this. If a school is to be judged, not unreasonably, on its academic results and status in league tables it is inevitable that this is where the school will focus its resources. But where does this leave the child who told her teacher that she had very bad toothache. The teacher looked to see if there was any obvious reason and saw that the child (aged 14) had rotten teeth. She contacted the family but was told that they were not able to use the dentist because they had failed to pay the bill when someone else in the family had been for treatment.

Some schools have support services that can assist students who lack support from their family or other sources. One London school is developing

153

bed spaces to provide accommodation for pupils who have been thrown out of home and are at risk of being on the streets. It is an extreme example but the clear alternative would be children who struggle to attend school because they have no home to go to at the end of the day. If the argument that we should 'hold on' to children both at home and at school is accepted then there is a clear case for investment in support services that are attached to schools.

One of the other causes of crime identified by many young offenders is boredom and the need for excitement. 'There is nothing to do, nowhere to go' was a common complaint. Looking for excitement has often been identified with group offending and also with gang membership. Both actually offer more than just a bit of excitement. They offer status, protection and friendships as well. Investment in some more constructive activities and some attractive places to go might make the difference between becoming involved in a crime and gang culture and becoming enthused and interested about some other activity. Projects across the country have offered wide ranging activities to engage young people. Sports projects, motor vehicle projects and arts-based projects all offer young people opportunities to try something different. At a Nacro project in Bradford the manager described a young man who had joined the scheme three weeks before:

> He came in with his mother. She did all the talking. He just sat there huddled up in his hoodie. I went through all the activities that he might get involved with and that included a dance project we had at the time. She said he wouldn't like that but he did. Three weeks on he took part in a public performance. The dancing requires a lot of touching and a lot of trust and he did brilliantly. He was like a different guy. He stood up tall, he looked confident and in control and he was talking happily about what he got from the project. It was a complete transformation.'

It is almost a cliché that the way out of a poor background has been sport or music. Perhaps only the most talented and most fortunate are offered a career this way but there are many who will not only become motivated through the activity itself but will also experience good, responsible adults with whom they can have a positive relationship.

154

Relationships with adults do appear to be key for many young offenders. Many of them have spoken about the difference it has made to them when they have an adult who cares about them and listens to them. Many have also experienced very negative responses from adults. Lack of social skill and lack of language ability may lead some young people to appear aggressive and insolent. We hear a great deal about the arrogant insolence of young people. There tends to be less awareness of the importance of the language and social skills of the adults who deal with young people. Young offenders have commented on the dismissive way they were treated by teachers, by staff in benefits offices and housing offices and by the police officers who stop and search them. Sometimes the aggressive behaviour displayed by the young person is a, not unreasonable, response to being treated badly by an adult. One prison governor, taking over the management of a YOI arranged for the staff to have training in dealing with adolescents. It would reduce some of the conflict between young offenders and authority figures if those authority figures were better equipped to deal with adolescent behaviour and to accept that the young person who is behaving badly or appears to be rude just might have problems or might be frightened about what is going to happen to them.

The ideal should be to keep young people out of the criminal justice system and to avoid them getting a criminal record, even if they do become involved in minor crime. Dealing with offences outside of the system means that there is none of the longer term damage that comes from the fact of a record. The best of community policing is where a local officer is able to have a quiet word and ask what is going on, sometimes being able to refer a young person to services that they need. So much recent evidence points to the value of inter-agency referral and the benefits of collaborative and well co-ordinated working practices. Early identification of problems, good assessment of the support that is needed and prompt responses in dealing with any issues can prevent a significant amount of offending and a significant number of young men from becoming involved in the criminal justice system. Inevitably though there will be some young men who are dealt with through that system and for whom an appearance in court will follow.

The use of community-based penalties has always been fraught with perceptions about 'people getting away with something'. Press reports of trials refer to the defendant 'walking free from court' and this contributes to the perception that once a crime comes before the court the only real penalty is a prison sentence, anything else is 'being let off'. In fact many community penalties can be as demanding and challenging as the most obviously severe sentences. Restorative justice is an example. For a young man who has shown little awareness of the impact of his actions on other people and has acted thoughtlessly and recklessly a meeting with a victim is a challenging and chastening experience.

Tony was a pleasant and engaging young man who lived with his father. His mother had died when he was quite small. He was still at school and was doing reasonably well but he appeared in court charged with stealing cigarettes from the local store. He had not given any thought to the person who ran the store so the meeting between them came as something of a shock. After the meeting he said,

> That was a real shock to me. I never really thought about a person running the shop. It was a business, it would be insured and all that. I never thought it would be a family, never thought about them being upset about it. Its been an eye opener. You won't get me doing that again.

When Joyce Evans was burgled and her TV set was stolen she was distraught. It was not just the loss, it was the sense that burglars had been in her house. She imagined big burly men breaking in and found it hard to sleep at night. When she met the culprit she found he was a 15-year-old who lived in a flat two floors below. He was embarrassed and apologetic and by the end of their conversation it seemed unlikely he would do the same thing again. Not only was the impact on this young offender profound but it also helped Mrs. Evans to get over the experience and to sleep soundly again.

The approach can work for groups and communities as well. In one neighbourhood the police had received numerous complaints from local residents about young people playing football on the communal grass area at the centre of the housing estate. Rather than simply move the young people on, the response involved a meeting of all the people involved and affected. This meant that older residents and young footballers met each other and could share their concerns. The result in this case was spectacularly positive. The local community realised that they must offer somewhere for young people to go and began to fund raise for a local facility. Many of the young people started doing the shopping for older and less mobile residents. Proper communication had broken down stereotypes and improved understanding on both sides.

Restorative justice will not provide the answer for every young offender. There is no one solution that will suit every offender. It is, however, an approach that sits more easily with a welfare-based approach to dealing with crime than a punishment based retributive model.

The reasons for involvement in crime are likely to be peculiar to an individual. For some young men their criminal phase is exactly that, a short term phase soon grown out of and usually regretted. Some will have help in growing out either through informal means such as friends, family or teachers. Some will be helped through the intervention of a statutory agency. Some will not be ready to change. These are the young men who are at risk of a custodial sentence.

Where prison appears to be the only suitable response it is crucial that the prison environment is one that offers real opportunity to learn new skills and to be prepared for life in the community after release. There are a number of reasons for any prisoner to take advantage of constructive activities on offer. It may help in the earning of privileges and so an improved environment and at the very least it is a chance to be out of their cell and meeting a few other people. Courses which challenge aspects of offending behaviour allow for the development of new skills and help in improving employability all contribute to mitigating the damage of custody. However, the provision of such activities is not consistent and the availability of opportunity is much diminished if there are fewer resources in the prison. Forster pointed out in 1987 that there are a number of practical constraints. Security and regime requirements affect the hours when activities can take place, the use of materials and whether a prisoner will complete a course or be transferred to another establishment. The best of regimes will be vulnerable to a security crisis. An escape, or even the threat of an escape or incident, can result in prisoners being kept in their cells for long periods. Staff sickness, reduced resources and efficiency savings all impact on the regime that can be provided. All these constraints are greater when the prison population is high and the available resources are therefore stretched. Efforts to keep the prison population down are essential if prisons are to be able to provide regimes that genuinely contribute to a reduction in offending.

Responses through a criminal justice system and through prison sentences are inevitably about 'picking up the pieces'. By the time a young person is involved in the system they have already done harm to others and to themselves. Constructive regimes may help but there will always be limitations to their effectiveness. However much can be done in a prison to mitigate the damage that has been done in the past and has been done through life in the institution, there remains a serious risk that the effort and the resources will be wasted in the traumatic days after release.

The most vulnerable prisoners leaving custody will need support. These are young people for whom there will have been little support throughout their lives. The evidence would suggest that this is one of the reasons for their involvement in crime. Leaving custody can mean that a young person needs to find somewhere to live and buy all the necessities to live in it. They will do this on limited income and without experience of setting up a home of any sort. They will need to find work, to access benefits. They will need to comply with licence conditions. This is expecting a lot of a young person. Most responsible parents will say that there is a great deal of support required in bringing up a child. Not just when they are tiny and obviously hugely dependent but right the way through to adulthood. How many times do parents provide transport, lend money, give advice? Who buys the food for the household? Who pays the bills? Who does most of the washing and the cleaning? Remove all those 'services' and how many young people would find it easy to manage on their own?

We need to make sure that all young people leaving custody have access to support in some form that will help to replicate the support that their more fortunate peers receive from their parents. There is an obvious resource implication in this but without the support the risks of failure are high. That is to be avoided if we want to reduce the risk of re-offending and we want to protect the public but it is surely more important that we give young people second chances and make it possible and practical for them to live successful and law-abiding lives.

They will not be able to do that if, despite their best efforts, they are rejected. Rejected by employers, by landlords, by credit companies, by insurance brokers and by their families. Our expectations of young offenders must be realistic. It is important to accept and acknowledge that young people who have had a singularly poor start in life will find it hard to change the lifestyle that they know. It has been abundantly clear that punishment alone is not enough, even where behaviour is completely unacceptable. Parents who dealt with a small child by means of punishment alone would be considered cruel and sadistic. Most parents may impose a punishment for misbehaviour but they will also offer the opportunity for rehabilitation and forgiveness. A welfare model which takes into account the life experiences of the young person must surely be both more humane and more effective

A change to any such model is, inevitably, controversial. There will always be some calls for more severe sentences, a demand for revenge and retribution. However, the evidence is that an informed and educated public, a public which does not have a disproportionate fear of crime, is less likely to make those punitive demands. Equally, there will be arguments against the investment required in order to achieve the support for families and young children, which is crucial to this model. Yet the cost of a full time worker with a family for 12 months would cost less than keeping a young person in custody for the same amount of time if we only compare the relative costs of the two responses. The price of the services provided is very much the tip of the iceberg. The financial costs of a criminal career are extensive. Police time, court time, probation time, insurance claims and financial loss to individuals. The emotional cost of a criminal career, in terms of damage to victims and communities, is incalculable.

The young offenders who have contributed their comments in this book have not denied that their own behaviour has been difficult. They do not deny that their offences warranted some punishment. They agree that the decision to stop offending is a personal one and that no amount of help will dissuade the determined criminal. What they do say is that there have been people, situations and circumstances in their lives, which have made it harder for them not to offend and harder to stop offending. Faced with a similar life history how many of us could be absolutely sure that we would not have taken a similar path and how many of us would be grateful for help, support and encouragement to overcome disadvantage and become responsible members of a community? Would most of us not want a second chance, an opportunity to overcome past mistakes and to do things differently in the future?

These are young people who have started life from a position of disadvantage. From that starting point they have made mistakes and they have done some wrong. They have also experienced trauma, hardship and unfairness. They have been abused and failed by parents, schools and systems. They have been judged and found wanting and have been treated with prejudice and distaste, sometimes by the very people who should have helped them. How can it possibly be right or fair that a young man in his late teens should be saying,

> No-one has ever said they were proud of me before.

In a society where it seems that government policy is increasingly determined on the playing fields of Eton it is more important than ever that we recognise that not all young people are born equal or treated equally. We must accept a responsibility for those who face disadvantage and do what we can to mitigate and eliminate that disadvantage in order to help some of our most vulnerable young citizens. If society needs a reward for that it may well find it in a reduction in youth crime.

REFERENCES AND BIBLIOGRAPHY

Askew S and Ross C, 1988, *Boys Don't Cry: Boys and Sexism in Education,* Buckingham: Open University Press.

Allen G, 2011, 'Early Intervention: The Next Steps'.

Barrow Cadbury Commission Report. 'Lost in Translation', 2005.

Bernstein B, 1962, 'Social Class, Linguistic Codes and Grammatical Elements', *Language and Speech,* 5 31-46.

Blumstein A, Cohen J and Nagin D (eds.) (1978), *Deterrence and Incapacitation,* Washington DC: National Academy Press.

Canaan J E, 1996, 'One Thing Leads to Another: Drinking, Fighting and Working Class Masculinities', in *Understanding Masculinities,* Mairtin Mac An Ghaill (ed.), Milton Keynes: Open University Press.

Chambliss W J, 1975, 'The Saints and the Roughnecks', in *Society,* Vol.11.

Cohen S, 1972, *Folk Devils and Moral Panics: The Creation of the Mods and Rockers,* London: MacGibbon and Kee.

Coleman J S, 1961, *The Social Life of A Teenager and Its Impact on Education,* New York: The Free Press.

Collier R, 1998, *Masculinities Crime and Criminology,* London: Sage.

Connell R, 1987, *Gender and Power: Society, The Person and Social Politics,* Cambridge: Polity Press.

Crutchfield R, 1995, 'Ethnicity, Labour Markets and Crime.' In DF Hawkins (ed.), *Ethnicity, Race and Crime.* 194-211, Albany, NY: State University of New York Press.

Dawson P, 2007, Home Office Online Report 09/07, 'The National PPO Evaluation – Research to Inform and Guide Practice', http://library.npia.police.uk/docs/hordsolr/rdsolr0907.pdf (last accessed 15 January 2012).

Dawson P and Cuppleditch L, Home Office Online Report 08/07, 'Impact Assessment of the Prolific and other Priority Offender Programme', http://library.npia.police.uk/docs/hordsolr/rdsolr0807.pdf (last accessed 15 January 2012).

Devlin A, 1995, *Criminal Classes,* Winchester: Waterside Press.

Duguid S and Pawson R, 'Education, Change and Transformation: The Prison Experience', *Evaluation Review,* Vol.22, No. 4, August 1998, Sage Publications.

Emler N and Reicher S, 1995, *Adolescence and Delinquency,* Oxford: Blackwell.

Erikson E H, 1968, *Youth and Crisis,* New York: Norton.

Farrington D P, 1973, 'Self Reports of Deviant Behaviour: Predictive and Stable?', *Journal of Criminal Law and Criminology,* 64, pp.99-110.

Farrington D P, 1996, *Understanding and Preventing Youth Crime,* Published by YPS for the Joseph Rowntree Foundation.

Farrington D and West D P, 1973 *Second Report of the Cambridge Study in Delinquent Development,* Heinneman: London.

Forster W, 1987, 'Towards a Prison Curriculum', in L Morin (ed.), 1987, *On Prison Education,* Canada: Canadian Government Publishing Centre.

Freud A, 1952, 'Adolescence', *Psychoanalytical Study of the Child,* Vol.13, pp.255-78.

Goffman E, 1968, *Asylums,* Harmondsworth, Penguin.

Guardian, December 8, 2010.

Graham J and Bowling B, 1995, *Young People and Crime,* Home Office Research Study, No.145, London: HMSO.

Head J, 1999, *Understanding the Boys: Issues of Behaviour and Achievement,* London: Falmer Press.

Hirschi T, 1969, *The Causes of Delinquency,* Berkeley LA: University of California Press.

Home Office 2007: see Dawson P; Dawson P and Cuppleditch L.

Hood R, 1992, *Race and Sentencing: A Study in the Crown Court,* London: Clarendon Press.

Hughes E, 2000, 'An Inside View: Prisoners' Letters on Education', in Wilson D and Reuss A, *Prison(er) Education,* Winchester: Waterside Press.

IPPR Report, 'Make Me A Criminal' 2008.

Jefferson T, 1992, 'Men and Crime', *Achilles Heel,* Issue 13, Summer.

Justice, 1996, *Children and Homicide: Appropriate Procedures for Juveniles in Murder and Manslaughter Cases,* London: Justice.

Keating D P, 1988, 'Adolescent Thinking', in S S Feldman and G R Elliot (eds.), *At the Threshold: The Developing Adolescent,* Cambridge MA: Harvard University Press, 54-89.

Kellmer Pringle, 1971, *Deprivation and Education,* London: Longman Group Ltd.

Kolvin I, Miller F J W, Fleeting M and Kolvin P A, 1988 'Social and Parenting Factors Affecting Criminal Offence Rates: Findings from the Newcastle Thousand-Family Study' (1947-1980), *British Journal of Psychiatry*, 152 pp 80-90.

Lovbakke J, 2007, 'Public Perceptions', in S Nicholas, C Kershaw and A Walker (eds.), *Crime in England and Wales 2006/7*, London: Home Office Research, Development and Statistics Directorate.

McCara L and McVie S, 2007 'Youth Justice? The Impact of System Contact on Patterns of Desistance from Offending'. *European Journal of Criminology.*

McGuire J, 2002, 'Criminal Sanctions Versus Psychologically Based Interventions With Offenders: A Comparative Empirical Analysis', *Psychology, Crime and Law,* 8 183-208.

McGuire J, 'Comparing Coercive and Non-coercive Interventions', Centre for Crime and Justice Studies. 'Transition to Adulthood', February 2010.

McIvor G, Jamieson J and Murray C, 2000, 'Study Examines Gender Differences in Desistance from Crime', *Offender Programmes Report,* Vol.4 No.1 5-9.

Mandela N, 1998, in Stern V, *A Sin Against the Future: Imprisonment in the World,* London: Penguin.

Marcia J, 1966, 'Development and Validation of Ego-Identity Status', *Journal of Personality and Social Psychology,* 3 551-58.

Maruna S, 2000, 'Desistance from Crime and Offender Rehabilitation: A Tale of Two Research Literatures', *Offender Programmes Report,* Vol.4 No.1, 1-13.

Maruna S and Immarigeon R, 2004 (eds), *After Crime and Punishment: Pathways to Offender Re-integration,* Cullompton: Willan.

Matza D, 1964, *Delinquency and Drift,* London: John Wiley and Sons.

Maughan B, Pickles A, Hagell A, Rutter M and Yule W, 1996, 'Reading Problems and Anti-Social Behaviour: Developmental Trends in Commorbidity', *Journal of Child Psychology and Psychiatry,* 37 405-18.

Mays J B, 1959, *On the Threshold of Delinquency,* Liverpool: Liverpool University Press.

Muncie J, 1999, *Youth and Crime: A Critical Introduction,* London: Sage Publications.

Nacro, 1986, 'Black People in the Criminal Justice System'.

Nacro, 1989, 'Race and Criminal Justice: The Way Forward'.

Nacro, 1992, 'Race Policies into Action'.

Nacro, 1999, 'Crossroads Project'.

Nacro, 1998, 'Wasted Lives'.

Nacro, 2000, 'On-Side Project Interim Evaluation Report' (unpublished).

Nacro, 2002, 'Young Prisoners' Views on the Prison System', Unpublished Research.

Narey, M 2001, Speech to the Howard League Conference.

Nettler G, 1974, *Explaining Crime,* New York, NY: Mcgraw-Hill.

Neustatter A, 2002, *Locked In Locked Out: The Experience of Young Offenders Out of Society and in Prison,* London: Calouste Gulbenkian Foundation.

Newson J and Newson E, 1989, 'The Extent of Parental Physical Punishment in the UK', London: Approach.

Parker H J, 1974, *View From the Boys,* Newton Abbot: David and Charles Ltd.

Perry P, 2011, *Couch Fiction,* Palgrave McMillan.

Reuss A, 1999, 'Prison(er) Education', *The Howard Journal of Criminal Justice,* Vol.38, Number 2, May 1999, Oxford: Blackwell.

Rutherford A, 1995, *Growing Out of Crime: The New Era,* Waterside Press: Winchester.

Rutter M, Giller H and Hagel A, 1998, *Anti-Social Behaviour by Young People,* Cambridge: Cambridge University Press.

Rutter M, Maughn N, Mortimore P, Ouston J, with Smith A, 1979, *Fifteen Thousand Hours: Secondary Schools and their Effect on Children.*

Sammons P, Hillman T, Mortimore P, 1995, *Characteristics of Effective Schools: A Review of School Effectiveness Research,* International School Effectiveness and Improvement Centre, Institute of Education, University of London.

Sampson R J and Laub J H, 1993, *Crime in the Making: Pathways and Turning Points Through Life,* London: Harvard University Press.

Shaw S, 2001, *Listening to Young Prisoners: A Review of the Complaints Procedure by the Prisons Ombudsman,* London: HMSO.

Smith D J, 1995, 'Youth Crime and Conduct Disorders: Trends, Patterns and Causal Explanations' in M Rutter and D J Smith (eds.), *Psychosocial Disorders in Young People,* pp.389-489, Chichester: Wiley.

Smith D J, 2006 'Social Inclusion and Early Desistance from Crime. The Edinburgh Study of Youth Transitions and Crime'.

Social Exclusion Unit, 'Reducing Re-offending by Ex-prisoners', July 2002.

Stattin H and Klackeberg-Larson I, 'Early Language and Intelligence Development and their Relationship to Future Criminal Behaviour', *Journal of Abnormal Psychology 1990*, 102 369-78.

Stern V, 1998, *A Sin Against the Future: Imprisonment in the World*, London: Penguin.

Street Weapons Commission Report, 2008.

Theobold D and Farrington D, 2010, 'Why Do the Crime-reducing Effects of Marriage Vary with Age?', *British Journal of Criminology*, 51. 136-158.

Victim Support, 'Hoodie or Goodie? The Link Between Violent Victimisation and Offending in Young People; A Research Report'.

Wakefield S and Uggen C, 2008, 'Having a Kid Changes Everything? The Effects of Parenthood on Subsequent Crime', unpublished manuscript.

Walklate S, 1995, *Gender and Crime: An Introduction*, London: Prentice Hall Harvester Wheatsheaf.

Walsh C, 2010, 'Youth Justice and Neuroscience', *British Journal of Criminology*, 51 21=39.

Walsh F, 1982, 'Conceptualisation of Normal Family Functioning', in F Walsh (ed.), *Normal Family Processes*, New York: Guilford Press.

West D, 1982, *Delinquency: Its Roots Causes and Prospects*, London: Heinneman.

West D J, 1969, *Present Conduct and Future Delinquency: First Report of the Cambridge Study*, London: Heinneman.

West D J and Farrington D P, 1977, *The Delinquent Way of Life: Third Report of the Cambridge Study of Delinquent Development*, London: Heinneman.

Willis P, 1977, *Learning to Labour*, London: Saxon House.

Wilson D and Reuss A, 2000, *Prison(er) Education: Stories of Change and Transformation*, Winchester. Waterside Press.

Wilson H, 1980, 'Parental Supervision; A Neglected Aspect of Delinquency', *British Journal of Criminology*, 20, pp.203-35.

INDEX